For Jemma

Recip

from

Le Vieux Four

The Secret Culinary Adventures
of a Dorset Pastry Chef

Lynette Fisher

Lynette

Illustrations Marion Taylor
ipad doodles by the author

ISBN 978-0-9927400-0-9

Published by Le Vieux Four Publishing, Beaminster, Dorset

Illustrations by Marion Taylor [http://www.dorsetpaintings.co.uk]

Design and typsetting by Border Typesetting, Beaminster, Dorset

Printed in Great Britain by iprint, Leicester

For Toby and Millie, the sneakiest cake thieves

A proportion of the profit from this book will be donated to the First Sight-Hound Rescue, and to Scruples Whippet Rescue

CONTENTS

Just a Few Sauces 70

Basic Pastry, Batters, Custards and Curds 77

Twenty-Two Years of Baking at *Le Vieux Four* 84

ACKNOWLEDGEMENTS

A big thank you to the thousands of customers who have come through the door of *Le Vieux Four* and told me not only how they have enjoyed my cooking, but also the unique atmosphere accompanied by a glimpse of life in a small Dorset town.

Thank you to those who come back loyally, time and time again, to find their favourite home-made treat instead of being wooed by the giant power of Marks and Spencer food hall or Waitrose.

Without your patronage *Le Vieux Four* would surely not still be trading after all these years, and I hope this book will carry on giving pleasure long after I have succumbed to the need for rest from my early morning baking.

FOREWORD

I first stumbled across *Le Vieux Four* when I escaped from London and came to live in Dorset, in the small village of Netherbury. Beaminster was my local town, and I will never forget walking down one of the wonky side streets and suddenly being hit by the most delicious aroma of freshly baked croissants. I followed my nose and there it was, plain to see, and I was suddenly transported to rural France. On stepping through the door it was a feast for the senses. Beautifully laid out tarts and pastries, all begging to be eaten. This was the first of many visits and I have often wished I was one of Lynette's students. Now she has put together this beautiful book of her wonderful recipes, I can indulge myself and my family to my heart's delight.

This is a book that I know has been a real passion for Lynette and without a doubt it will inspire its readers not only to visit her wonderful patisserie, but also to bake the inspirational recipes inside.

I know you will enjoy her recipes … happy cooking!

Lesley Waters

INTRODUCTION

*Take a spoonful of Provence, add a teaspoon of Dorset and mix well,
with herbs, spices and sea breezes*

This 'mélange' of recipes has become the essence of *Le Vieux Four* in Beaminster where, over time and with trial and error, I have developed my own specialties that perhaps people will remember when I finally hang up my pinny. Every recipe is only as good as the quality of the produce, and Dorset has much to offer.

Elizabeth David found such joy in all the specialties she discovered in her travels around the provinces of France; 'in Toulouse the beguiling crystallized violets, in Aix en Provence the exquisitely melting little almond cakes called calissons d'aix. And even in the most unexpected places in France one might find that there is a first class baker or confectioner'. I hope that people will remember a similar joy from my coeurs d'amande, my gateau basque, my Beaminster Buns and my Simnel cakes at Easter, carefully decorated with crystallised violets from Dorset gardens.

A teacher of mine in France once told me that anyone can be a good cook if they can follow a recipe carefully, add suitable touches of their own and not forget the importance of taste and simplicity, so never getting carried away by conflicting flavours or the desire to impress. I hope that these recipes are easy to grasp and that the cook who follows them can develop their own skills and ideas in bringing them to the table.

In our busy, stressful lives it is so important to make an occasion of every meal – even if it is simply a cake with a cup of tea or coffee, the care and attention to detail of a home-made treat brings immeasurable joy to cook and guest alike.

Ah, but of course my loyal customers, as you plough through my preface and flick on to the recipes, you may be forgiven for thinking 'well, has she never made all these things at *Le Vieux Four*', and this may be because you are unaware of my ocean-tramping history, of my toils to produce fine meals for celebrities in Cannes, oil magnates having a meeting in Bermuda, brain surgeons holidaying in the Caribbean, or simply my efforts to cheer a miserable crew mid-Atlantic with lopsided cakes from a sloping oven.

I started sailing with my father who shared a small wooden ketch called Anna, moored in the Beaulieu River. Here, I learnt to row amongst muddy banks, and remember falling half into the water while climbing onboard her slippery decks and thinking that perhaps my life was over, when in fact it was the beginning of the path I was to follow.

Later, after my parents' divorce, my stepfather Willy had a plywood catamaran moored in Mudeford, and to sail out over the Christchurch ledge pulling in five or six mackerel on one line became my passion. We sailed to Alderney, Guernsey and St Malo – my first taste of Sunday platters of seafood and homemade mayonnaise, and I was hooked. I had found my life's ambition; to sail and cook and eat. I purchased a tall wooden pepper grinder on our maiden voyage to Cherbourg, which has stayed by side all my working life!

Le Moulin au poivre noir

I first set out over stormy Atlantic seas to look for my grandfather, who had left my grandmother with three small children and sailed to St Lucia to purchase a small fishing business. He settled there away from the grand country life of hunting and shooting that he had always known, and when I finally arrived he was a terminally ill man in his eighties.

I had decided that in order to indulge my love of the sea and my quest to find grandfather Fisher I had to find a way to support myself through my adventures, so I embarked on a cookery diploma in London in my early twenties.

Fairly green in the kitchen, but diploma in hand, I flew to Spain and stayed with some friends on their beautiful charter yacht, Hawaita. They took me by sail to Gibraltar, as the border with Spain was still firmly closed, and from there I joined an American crew as a delivery cook bound for the Caribbean. I was not initially hired as cook, only as deck crew, but we encountered bad weather, the cook took to her bed and I filled her place on a full wage with return ticket. On arrival, the old whaling captain skipper asked me to stay on to sail north to Nantucket, but I had my heart set on charter cooking in the West Indies and so there I stayed.

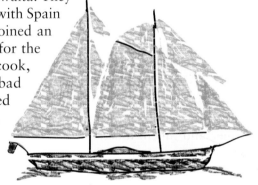

Hawaita

Luckily, I was soon part of the Nicholson charter crew and was delighted to be cooking while sailing the islands.

As well as the continuous problem of the instability of my kitchen, often I would seek out a local market in the hope of ingredients to inspire and would be faced with a pile of plantains and yams, so a grand menu never ceased to be a challenge.

Luckily we caught a great many fish and everywhere, on investigation, seemed to have its own specialties and recipes to make the best of the local produce available. With the help of local cookery books and experimentation, I struggled on, and many of those recipes have found their way in to this collection. I had brought with me an amusing amount of equipment, knives, garlic crushers, mixers, but perhaps the most unusual thing was my smoke box, which I will refer to later on among the recipes.

By chance, an American company heard of me cooking 'down islands' and summoned me to Fort Lauderdale for my dream job cooking on a sailing vessel, 103ft of sheer comfort and elegance. She was bound for Bermuda and then Europe and to return to sail the Antilles the following winter. There was some skepticism that this small sunburnt waif might not manage the weight of the saucepans, but I survived and stayed aboard for quite a few years.

Spending days at sea brings a wonderful sense of calm – all the rushing, shopping and stocking of freezers, fridges and cupboards, with all my endless lists, are quickly forgotten. The interests of the crew and guests alike focused on the weather, our route and, most importantly, the next meal and the snacks that might be on offer in between. Time seemed to stretch out through the days when no expeditions ashore were possible. I took my watches most of the time, to fit in with cooking, as I enjoyed the navigation and observation of other vessels. Sometimes someone else would cook and a break was appreciated especially when the weather was not kind.

During this time I at last found my grandfather, and we had a precious few hours together in which we wandered down to the sea for a swim and drank a glass of rum in a small bar. This was the first and only time we met, as he died shortly afterwards.

In the winters when we were not expected in the Caribbean the boat was docked in Antibes, and there I found the only place in the world I am truly at home. I was able to refresh my ideas with the most wonderful produce to hand, to eat in some of the simplest but finest restaurants in the world and to lurk amongst the beautiful patisseries I had ever seen.

In 1991 I became a landlubber and bought a derelict butcher's shop – a listed building with paper work back to the eighteenth century. It was cold, extremely dirty and in need of total renovation but the shop was open two weeks later in time for our first Christmas, and I have never looked back. Hidden down a side street in a very small town, its survival was shaky, but 22 years on little has changed although it is a little warmer and much, much cleaner. I still rise at 5am and cook as many tartelettes, cakes and sweet creations as I can to sell that day, as well as some savoury items for a light lunch or soup to warm cold winter walkers.

Did I ever have disasters, you may ask? Oh yes, the Christmas cake that had to be turned upside down and cut out from the bottom as the icing was too hard to cut, and the lemon curd that escaped from the tarts and had to be licked from the box, to admit to just two from a very long list!

I apologise for some French or even Spanish or Italian names for recipes, but sometimes they just do not sound right upon translation. Dorset Apple Cake with almonds is a Dorset treat with a French twist from an old recipe so it all becomes confused together into a Franglais in my head, as I try to write it all down. So maybe mixing the languages together is a good thing but not very grammatically correct, hence my apology before you read on.

A good friend once told me 'just because there are hundreds of cookery books out there, it does not mean there is not room for another one'.

So finally, here it is – another one …

OVEN TEMPERATURES

La Cocotte

Just a word about oven temperatures, the success of a recipe obviously depending on the right amount of cooking at the right heat.

When my recipe calls for a moderately hot oven this would equate to 150°C, a hot oven to 180–200°C, and a low oven to 100°C. I do find a fan-assisted electric oven more successful for choux pastry, brioche and mixtures that need to rise, set and cook right through, while the steady heat of gas on a slow temperature is guaranteed to keep a fruit cake moist. Aga cooking is a complete art learnt either by going to one of their smart cookery classes or, as in my case, by trial and error. The bottom oven is the best thing I have ever used for soups and stews, and I frequently bake sponge cakes and pastry in the top, but always with the baffle plate to prevent them burning.

MEASURING LIQUID

Sometimes it seems simpler, and saves me having to look for my glasses, to go without the measuring jug, and rather than a dash or a splash, which could be very hit and miss, I have used a receptacle to hand, sometimes a small wine glass = 125ml or a normal size mug = 200ml.

a dash of a splash?

SOUPS

panier au soupe

The winters can be cruel and long in Dorset compared to those I have known in the south of France, with too many grey and cold days when a bowl of soup with some fresh bread is the perfect remedy for a frozen soul. I have made and served all of these at *Le Vieux Four* and although some have a French twist about them all the ingredients are locally grown or caught!

A blender is an essential tool and patience is also necessary, as many soups taste better for long, slow cooking and a day or so of maturity.

SOUPE AU PISTOU

A hearty spring soup from Provence where in the market one can find the ingredients all chopped and ready in a bag with a large handful of basil sticking out of the top!

For 6 people:

2 large leeks

3 medium carrots

4 courgettes

a handful of fine green beans

200g soaked white haricot beans, or a small tin, which is simpler

4 large red tomatoes

2 cloves of garlic

1 tbsp olive oil

a large bunch of fresh basil, some celery leaves and parsley stalks

Sac au pistou

Peel and chop the tomatoes and place them in a heavy pan with the crushed garlic. Add the olive oil and cook this until the tomatoes are a purée.

Chop all the vegetables into small pieces, leaving the white haricot beans aside. Stir the vegetables into the garlic tomato mixture and add boiling water to cover. Finally add the haricot beans and put in the celery leaves and parsley stalks for added flavour. These can be removed before serving.

Season well with salt, and simmer the soup slowly – the bottom oven of an Aga is ideal. I always think that soupe au pistou is better after a day or so when the flavours have thoroughly merged.

After a few hours when the vegetables are soft, season to taste. Remove the celery leaves and parsley stalks if you have used them.

Chop the fresh basil and sprinkle generously on the soup to serve.

Finely chopped garlic and Parmesan can be added to the basil for stronger flavours, or a finely grated mature cheddar is a delicious too.

CELERIAC AND ALMOND SOUP

Ground almonds are often used in Provence to help thicken a soup.

For 6 people:
1 large celeriac root
2 medium leeks
2 large potatoes
2 tbsp ground almonds
toasted flaked almonds to garnish

Peel and chop the vegetables into chunks and cover with a light stock of chicken or vegetable. Bring to the boil and simmer gently until the vegetables are soft.

Blend the soup until smooth and add the ground almonds. Season to taste and serve the soup with the addition of a swirl of single cream and the toasted flakes of almond.

SOUPE DES BETTERAVES GLACE

Such a prettier word than beetroot, for such a pretty soup (and an easy one, too).

For 4 people:
400g cooked beetroot
a bunch of fresh chives
1 litre beef boullion
a cup crème frâiche

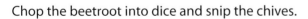

Chop the beetroot into dice and snip the chives.

Heat the beetroot in the bouillon for 20 minutes and season. Pass the soup through the blender and chill. Mix in the chives and crème fraîche.

Equally good hot as cold, but makes a lovely summer starter or lunch.

MINESTRONE

The name is taken from the Italian word minestra, which quite simply means a thick soup. Every good home cook from Cannes to Viareggio and then to Beaminster has their own recipe for this wonderful king of soups … here is mine.

For 6 people:
125g piece of poitrine fume – smoked belly lard
a small tin of white haricot beans
250g carrots
2 large leeks, the white part only
a branch of celery
500g potato
125g peas
1 small onion
3 pieces of garlic
40g butter
500g peeled chopped red tomatoes
60g rice or small pasta
fresh parsley and basil
a small handful of bitter salad such as endive (optional)

Soak the lard for 10 minutes and bring to the boil from cold, and throw away the water.

In a heavy pan cook the tomatoes in the butter until a purée with the crushed garlic.

Meanwhile, chop all the vegetables into small pieces, and the leek and onion into very fine rounds. Add them all to the pan with the cooked tomatoes and a tablespoon of chopped parsley and basil. Cover with 2 litres of hot water and let the soup steep for 20 minutes.

Add the lard and simmer for 1 hour. Add the peas and rice or pasta and cook for a further 2 minutes. Taste and season well.

This is traditionally almost a vegetable stew rather than a soup with very little spare liquid. Serve with a bowl of freshly grated cheese.

CREAMED APPLE SOUP

Outside our little local veg shop at the end of the summer Angie has a row of locally-grown apples in baskets and she can give you a wonderful description of how each one 'eats' as they say in Dorset. I often buy one from each basket … just to remind myself of their precious individuality.

I also have a huge Bramley tree in my garden and some years I have so many apples that I become innovative with their use, as, like my granny before me, waste is not an option!

For 4 people:
60g butter
120g finely chopped onion
500g peeled and chopped apples
600ml good chicken stock
150ml white wine

Melt the onions in the butter, add a teaspoon of curry powder and cook for 5 minutes. Add the apples and the wine, and simmer for 45 minutes.

Add the chicken stock, liquidise, sieve and serve.

This soup is equally good served chilled with the addition of a little cream. A squeeze of lemon may be added if sweet dessert apples have been used to sharpen the flavour.

SOUPE AUX MOULES A LA CRÈME

Fresh mussels are delicious, freshly available in Dorset when in season. I always soak them in some fresh water to make them spit out any sand they may be harbouring, then I discard any broken or cracked shells and clean them carefully pulling out their beards of weed.

For 4 people:
2kg mussels
100g butter
1 tbsp flour
2 glasses dry white wine
2 grated carrots
25ml crème frâiche
thyme, bay, celery and parsley sprigs to make a bouquet garni
black pepper

Place the mussels in a big heavy pan and heat them quickly until they open which takes 7 or 8 minutes. Discard any that remain tightly closed. Place the mussels in a colander, keeping they juice that they have produced to one side. Take the mussels from their shells, pinching them out carefully – using a shell itself as tweezers is a good way!

Melt the butter in the pan and sprinkle in the flour, mixing to a paste. Carefully add the white wine, mixing until smooth, with 4 glasses of water and the mussel juice. Add pepper, bouquet garni and the grated carrot. Cover and let this rest for 25 minutes for the flavours to blend.

Sieve the soup, replace the mussels and heat gently to serve without letting it boil. Finally, add the crème frâiche.

SOUPE A LA BASQUAISE

Several recipes from the Basque region have become firm favourites at Le Vieux Four, *and this hearty, tasty soup is simple and quick to make.*

For 4 people:

750g cod

3 onions

2 pieces of garlic

1 bouquet garni – parsley, celery, bay leaf and thyme

4 tbsp olive oil

salt and pepper

thyme

Peel the onions and mince them finely; crush the garlic with the blade of a knife or through a garlic press.

Heat the oil in a heavy pan and fry the onions gently until golden.

Add 1¼ litres of cold water, the garlic, bouquet garni and the seasoning. Cover the soup and let it boil for 15 minutes.

At the end of this time, cut the fish into pieces and add to the soup, cooking gently for an hour.

In the Basque they will often poach an egg in the cooking juices, thereby creating a complete meal.

for me please?

THE WEST BAY FISH SOUP

Across France there are several versions of the culinary masterpiece that is a tasty fish soup. In the south, a Bouillabaisse, indeed a meal in itself; from Brittany comes La Cotriade; La Bourride is the soup from the Midi and La Chaudree originates from the Atlantic coast.

With many a delicious catch being landed at West Bay, I decided our own personal recipe would be a very good idea.

For 4–5 people:
1.5kg of local fish, gurnard, dogfish, bream,
a small crab or 2, whiting or pout
3 large onions
4 cloves of garlic
4 large waxy potatoes
3 or 4 ripe tomatoes
2 tbsp tomato concentrate
bouquet garni
fennel
a piece of orange peel
3 pieces of saffron
golden slices of bread from the oven
rubbed with garlic

October Morning
Bridport

For a tasty rouille sauce:
6 cloves garlic
1 egg yolk
powdered saffron
cayenne pepper and sweet pimento powder
25ml olive oil

Clean, gut and descale the fish, wash, keep the heads and cut in chunks. Chop the onions finely and slice the peeled potatoes into rounds. Peel the tomatoes, scrape out the seeds and mash the flesh to a pulp. Peel and crush the garlic.

Put 2 tablespoons of olive oil in a heavy pan, or marmite as the French would call it, and place in the rounds of potato, the onions, the bouquet garni, the fennel and the orange peel. Place all the fish and the crabs onto this base, placing the most delicate fish on the surface. Now add the tomato pulp, the concentrate and all the seasonings; sprinkle with the rest of the olive oil and allow to rest in the fridge for 2–3 hours.

Before cooking, set the delicate fish aside and pour 3 litres of boiling water over the rest. Bring to the boil for 15 minutes, replace the other fish and cook for a further 5 minutes.

To prepare the rouille, put the crushed garlic, having removed the shoot, in a bowl with a little salt and mix with a few drops of olive oil until smooth. Add the egg yolk and incorporate the oil little by little as for mayonnaise, with a small whisk or a fork. When the sauce is firm add the seasonings.

To serve, carefully lift the fish and serve on a large warm serving dish with the potato. Sieve the bouillon and serve the soup alongside the fish, giving your guests large pasta bowls so they can incorporate the bouillon and the fish and spread the rouille on freshly made croutons from the oven.

PEA AND HAM

A favourite at Le Vieux Four *on those dark, winter days by the fire.*

For 6 people:
500g piece of rolled gammon
4 tins of petits pois

Cover the gammon with cold water and bring to the boil. Throw this water away and place the gammon in a heavy pan with a fresh covering of water, bring to simmering point and then allow to cook long and slowly. I place mine in a Le Creuset-type dish in the bottom oven of the Aga over night. This gives a perfect heat. When the gammon is cooked it should be tender enough to shred with a fork.

Take the meat out of the cooking liquor and set to one side. Strain and liquidize the petits pois, adding the cooking liquor to the blender. Replace the resulting soup in the pan and shred in the gammon in manageable pieces, removing any fat or gristle carefully.

Taste the soup and season with freshly ground black pepper.

Garnish the soup with plenty of chopped parsley.

MUSHROOM SOUP

A favourite to use up those mushrooms which look a little tired, and also that loaf of ciabatta or similar that looks a little stale.

For 6 people:
1kg mushrooms
1 loaf stale ciabatta or similar
2 litres of light stock
butter
a clove of garlic
seasoning
a small cup of cream
milk to thin the soup to taste

Sweat the mushrooms in a heavy pan with the crushed garlic and butter. Meanwhile, soak the bread in some of the stock.

Cook the mushrooms until soft and black with the juices running.

Incorporate all the ingredients together in a blender and add a splash or two of milk if the soup is too thick.

Reheat the soup and season well to serve, with salt and freshly ground black pepper. A little cream makes the soup wonderfully rich and creamy.

SOUP OF 3 GREENS

Sorrel has a wonderful unique flavour, in a soup or sauce for fish, and grows quite tenaciously in my garden, so it seems to like Dorset. A tasty summer soup that is quick to make.

For 4 people:

12 leaves of spinach

12 leaves of sorrel

1 lettuce

80g butter

½ cup crème frâiche

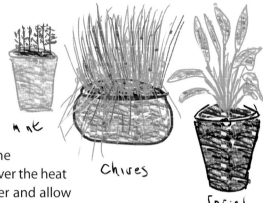

Wash and chop all the leaves, melt the butter in heavy pan and toss the leaves over the heat for 5 minutes. Add 1¼ litres of cold water and allow to simmer for 30 minutes.

Season well to taste and stir in the crème frâiche. Serve immediately.

ONION SOUP *Le Vieux Four* WAY

I only seem to make onion soup in the winter when the Aga is alight as the long slow cooking overnight in the bottom oven is essential to extract the wonderful sweetness of the onions.

For 4 people:

6 medium size onions

1½ litres beef stock

Peel and slice the onions into thin rounds. Place them in a heavy pan and cook them in a little oil, stirring frequently until soft and beginning to take colour but being careful not to burn them.

Pour the boiling stock over them and transfer into a slow oven for 6–8 hours. Now the soup will be a golden shimmering brown with the onions melting as you taste.

Season well.

Serve with grated cheese and croutons.

CREAMY ASPARAGUS SOUP

In Beaminster we have an abundance of local asparagus in late spring and this soup, to use up the not so special bunches, concentrates the flavour to perfection.

For 4 people:

2 bunches of fresh local asparagus

2 litres light stock

a stale ciabatta

Chop the ends of the asparagus, just the very last inch of stalk, and simmer the bunches in the stock until tender. Soak the ciabatta in 2 ladles of the hot stock.

Blend the asparagus and then sieve the soup back into the pan so all the stringy bits are discarded, but none of the flavour! Blend the ciabatta, adding a little of the soup to make it smoother, and then add this to the pan. Reheat and season; add cream and chopped parsley to serve.

ACCOMPANIMENTS TO SOUP

Thick Parmesan biscuits

Especially good with chilled soups, but good with hot ones too.

For 12 biscuits of 1" diameter:
220g flour
50g each of butter and grated Parmesan
1 egg yolk
salt and cayenne pepper

Rub the butter into the flour and add the cheese, egg and seasonings. Moisten with a very little water if necessary, to facilitate rolling.

Cut into rounds or shapes 2cm thick. Bake in a moderate oven for 20 minutes.

Flavoured butter baguettes

We always have baguette hanging around that is past its best, which, when popped back into the oven filled with a flavoured butter, is just delicious with soups, salads, pasta dishes, stews or just on its own, or to fill a hungry hole whilst waiting for a dish to cook.

I cut the baguette in slices of about 3cms but not quite slicing it through, carefully spread the butter on one side of each slice and wrap the whole in foil, leaving the top open to let the baguette crisp on the top. Five to ten minutes in a hot oven should melt the butter and refresh the baguette.

Obviously the favourite butter is garlic but herb butters are delicious too, especially parsley or chervil. Anchovy butter is also a tasty choice.

Gougère

A specialty from Burgundy – basically cheesy choux pastry – exceptionally good warm from the oven with a bowl of soup.

¼ litre water
125g of butter
4 eggs
125g of Emmental or Gruyère
salt and freshly ground black pepper

Tip the water into a saucepan and add the butter cut into pieces. Melt the butter and bring to the boil. Take the pan off the heat and quickly add the sieved flour, stirring until a smooth paste is obtained. Place back on the heat and, stirring continuously, drive out the steam until the mixture comes away cleanly from the sides of the pan.

Remove from the heat, allow the mixture to cool a little and then add the eggs one by one, stirring vigorously until the paste is shiny. Add the cheese, cut into dice, and the seasonings.

Prepare a tray with baking paper and pipe the mix with a large nozzle into a round crown shape with a second layer on top. Brush lightly with beaten egg to glaze and bake in a hot oven for 20 minutes, then turn the oven down for a further 10 minutes to harden the pastry.

Serve warm.

FAVOURITE SUPPERS AND LUNCHES

Much of my time as a charter cook at sea was spent menu writing, trying to always have a plan, even if circumstance caused me to abandon it, maybe in favour of a fish that had been caught, or something in a local market that caught my eye as being the perfect dish for the day. Having laboriously mapped out a day to day list of dishes, even with details of the cake to bake for tea, I began each day with confidence and no horrible 'what on earth shall I cook today feeling' which was definitely to be avoided at all costs.

On the stern deck of Fei Seen was a wide bench seat, a favourite fishing spot, and there I would sit as we were chased across the Atlantic Ocean by the trade winds or bounced across the Mediterranean by the Mistral, endlessly deciding what to cook for crew and guests alike.

Of course I had a huge deep freeze, large enough to hold a body in fact in case some poor soul should leave us on passage, but then what would I have done with all the wonderful joints of meat, fish, poultry and delicious collection of cheeses that I had squirreled away for our sojourn in the islands?

I had a larder cupboard that I would provision carefully with all the basic ingredients and many more tins of special delicacies to help with adding a zing to a starter or exciting a dull salad, when there was little or nothing to be found ashore. I grew herbs inside the crew hatch where they would be sheltered from salty spray and even resorted to growing bean sprouts in a jar, somewhere where there was little salad to be seen.

All of the following suppers and lunches were made time and time again, along with of course many more, and I wish I had kept the original menu lists although I have come across a couple from time to time, slipped into a cook book or recipe file.

All of the following recipes feed 4–6 people unless otherwise stated.

FISH

One of the most charming moments in my culinary career, was when the five year old grandson of one of my customers came into the shop and said "because you make such yummy cakes I've caught you some fish" and presented me with 5 glistening fresh mackerel caught early off Cogden Beach. In June the mackerel run thick and fast off the Jurassic coast and there are usually plenty to be had by all.

Cooking fresh fish has been an important part of my life, sitting on the bathing ladder gutting the catch of a proud crew member or guest in order to present it later at the table to be admired and enjoyed almost as much as the fishing and catching.

So many different fish from all the oceans I have sailed and I am amazed at how the lobsters caught off the Dorset coast look so totally different to those we brought aboard in the Caribbean islands. I became used to adapting recipes to suit each fish depending on the flavour and texture and my decision as to which family it belonged.

MACKEREL EN PAPILLOTE

With an abundance of these fish caught off the Dorset coast every year, they make a wonderful early summer meal. 'En papillotte' describes the butterfly-shaped piece of foil in which the fish is wrapped.

Take one good sized mackerel for each person and cut a heart or butterfly-shaped piece of foil in which to wrap each one.

Gut and wash the fish, either leaving the head on or removing it, whichever you prefer. Butter each piece of foil and lie a fish on each one.

Mix together in a small bowl:
1 teacup chopped parsley
½ cup chopped capers
60g butter
cayenne, salt and black pepper

Season the inside of the fish and place a little of the butter mixture in each. Fold the foil over the fish and crimp the edges together so that none of the cooking juices can escape, and bake in a hot oven for 25–30 minutes. Alternatively, these little fish parcels cook very well on the barbeque.

Serve in the parcel for your guests to open as all the wonderful juices and aromas are trapped inside and need only a wedge of lemon for perfection.

Maquereau mariné.

SOUSED MACKEREL

A real favourite of mine that keeps for a few days in the fridge and improves with time. This recipe from Larousse Gastrominique is simple and perfect.

Put a layer of finely sliced onions and carrots in an oval earthenware dish with sprigs of parsley and thyme, half a bay leaf, a few peppercorns and one or two cloves. Lie the cleaned headless fish on the vegetables. Pour over them a mix of white wine and white wine vinegar in equal parts. This should not quite cover them. Put another layer of sliced onions and carrots on top, and cover the dish with oiled paper. Bring to the boil and simmer for 15 minutes. Cool the fish in the stock and refrigerate; drain to serve.

PESCE IN SAOR

This recipe comes from Venice, where I was lucky enough to work for two memorable summers. I would go to the butcher and fishmonger very early in the morning and they would wheel my purchases back to the quay in huge wooden wheelbarrows, and their joviality and helpfulness was refreshing. Italians do wonderful things with fish and I have made this many times when we have had a glut of Dorset mackerel.

1kg mackerel
1kg white mild onions
3 wine glasses olive oil
3 wine glasses white wine
vinegar
flour
salt, pine nuts and pieces of lemon peel

Gut and behead the fish. Flour and fry the fish or grill them.

Fry the sliced onions until a golden colour, pour in the vinegar and reduce a little. Add the sultanas, pine nuts and bits of lemon peel.

Fill an earthenware pot with alternating layers of fish and onions, removing bones and skin. Add the cooking liquor and be careful to finish with a layer of onions. Chill for a day or two before serving.

SARDINES PANE

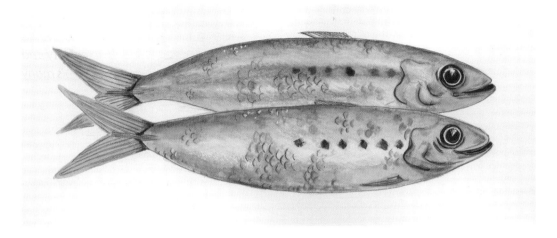

When I was born, my brother Edmund had difficulty saying my name so I became Nette to everyone. Unfortunately this stuck through school and beyond, although only family and old friends use it now. Net in French means clean and tidy and my mother spotted a pot for the table in Antibes market with my name emblazoned on the front, so of course she could not resist buying it for me. The real purpose of this pot of course is to keep the table tidy, a dustbin for sardine tails, mussel shells and general refuse from our plates at table. It now proudly adorns my kitchen, after some thirty years of service.

A speciality Antiboise and a great favourite aboard ship, this is the simplest way to cook these little fish that are just as available caught off the Jurassic coast in Dorset.

Cut off the heads of some very fresh, gutted sardines and place the belly side down on a board. Press a finger firmly along the backbone to flatten the fish and then the bones will lift easily out from the belly side. Leave the tails, as they make the fish look attractive when arranged around a plate to serve and also to give you something to hold onto when dipping and crumbing the fish.

Dip the sardines first in beaten egg and then into fine fresh breadcrumbs. Pan fry in hot vegetable oil for a couple of minutes each side until golden, and drain on adsorbent paper.

Serve immediately with wedges of fresh lemon.

TABLE NETTE

SARDINES FARCI

Prepare the sardines as in the preceding recipe.

For 12 sardines:
200g breadcrumbs
75g finely chopped onion
20g finely chopped shallot
2 tbsp white wine
100g finely chopped mushrooms
1 tbsp chopped parsley
2 eggs
lemon juice and seasonings

Soak the breadcrumbs in milk, squeeze out the excess and stir them in a bowl. Cook the finely chopped onion in butter until soft.

Cook the shallot in the white wine until all the liquid has evaporated. Add these to the breadcrumbs, along with the mushrooms and a tablespoon of chopped parsley.

Mix the stuffing together with the eggs and a squeeze of lemon, and season with salt, black pepper and nutmeg. Place a teaspoon of the stuffing on each sardine and roll it up towards the tail, securing each with a cocktail stick.

Bake in a moderate oven for 20 minutes, after which time the cocktail stick can be removed and the little parcels will keep their shape.

Serve hot with a homemade tomato sauce with crushed garlic and plenty of freshly chopped basil.

MOUSSE ALBERT

On my travels I had in my equipment (you would not have believed my baggage of cook books, cake tins and the rest!) a smoke box and a bag of oak sawdust to place in the bottom. The box stood on a little rack with 2 burners of methylated spirit underneath. With this unlikely piece of apparatus I could smoke fish, chicken, nuts or anything else as the fancy took me, which it frequently did. I can remember the first time I smoked some fish on the quayside in English Harbour, Antigua, much to the fascination of the local lads.

In Bridport we have a wonderful local smokery so I do not have to go to these lengths to procure the smoked mackerel needed to make this tasty mousse.

For 6–8 people:
3 smoked mackerel
2 apples
45g butter
juice of 2 lemons
1 cup double cream
1 tbsp horseradish sauce
salt and pepper
4 leaves of gelatine
4 egg whites

Dissolve the leaf gelatine in a little water in the microwave or over a bowl of hot water. Stir until clear. Peel and core the apples, and slice into the lemon juice to avoid discolouration. Cook until soft in the butter and lemon juice.

Fillet the fish, removing all the bones, and in a blender or food processor, combine the fish, apple, gelatine, horseradish and seasoning. When this mixture is cool, softly whip the cream and fold in gently. Chill until half set and then fold in the stiffly-beaten whites. Chill until set.

To serve, chop well-grilled bacon and scatter on the top. A lively rocket and watercress salad complements the mousse very well.

FILETS DE SOLE A L'ORANGE

A lovely light lunch dish with plenty of local sole available in Dorset. The local fisherman bring up nets and nets of plaice, but nestling amongst them sometimes there are sole, the jewel of the catch.

600g sole fillets
10ml dry white wine
1 lemon
1 orange
2 carrots
1 small fennel bulb
1 tsp paprika
1 tbsp chopped parsley
salt and pepper

Wash the sole fillets and dry them. Place them in an ovenproof dish. Dampen them with the wine and an additional 10ml of water. Season and cook for 5 minutes in the oven.

Peel the carrots and the fennel bulb and chop them to a fine mixture, in a food processor if possible. Cut half of the zest of the orange into very fine strips. Take the sole from the oven and add the chopped vegetable mix, the juice of the lemon, parsley, orange zest and paprika. Cook again for 5 minutes in a hot oven.

Arrange the sole fillets and the chopped vegetable mix on a serving dish with the cooking juices, and decorate with rounds of orange.

Le plat au poisson

MOULES A LA BORDELAISE

A grand recipe for mussels … I do find that all the restaurants around Beaminster tend to always cook mussels à la marinière or similar and sometimes it's good to be a little more adventurous.

I had a bumpy ride with a small wooden sailing boat down the Garonne River many years ago, and came to rest in Bordeaux for repairs. They winched the boat out of the water on a wooden cradle that creaked and groaned and took a very long time, with the boat lurching at every tug of the wire. When they came to the re-launch however, they simply released the brake and we hurtled down to hit the water with a very undignified splash. I have never been quite so scared as on that ride down the slipway, sad to admit to not ever being an Alton Towers enthusiast. The trip down the river with its local tidal bore wave was adventurous enough too, but the food made up for all the misdemeanors of the area by being superb.

1kg mussels
1 large onion
1 good red carrot
3 shallots
1 tbsp flour
50ml white wine from Bordeaux
½ tsp crushed black pepper
1 tbsp tomato purée
80g of butter
salt, pepper and chopped parsley

Peel and chop the onion, shallots and carrot, and soften them over a gentle heat in a little of the butter. Stir them with a wooden spoon and do not let them take colour. Sprinkle with the flour, and let the mixture cook a little, moisten with the wine, add the black pepper and let this cook over a tiny flame for 20 minutes. This sauce, gently reduced, will be fairly thick.

Clean the mussels, scrape them and pull out the beards. Open them over a fast flame with the rest of the white wine, stirring to distribute the heat. Strain the mussels when they are open and sieve the cooking juices. Discard the empty half of the shell and keep the mussels warm.

Mix the tomato concentrate with the mussel stock and stir this into the reduced sauce. Leave to allow the flavours to mingle for 10 minutes, taste to adjust the seasonings and stir in the rest of the butter cut into small pieces. Reheat the mussels in this sauce but do not boil. Sprinkle liberally with chopped parsley to serve.

DAURADE FARCI A LA PROVENCALE

Stuffed red bream, as it is prepared in the south of France, is a dish of mouthwatering freshness and flavours. Many of the old restaurants in the small streets of Antibes and other towns in this area have a huge wood oven, the stone arch of the mouth often visible to the diners. Out of these ovens come delectable pizzas, tartes aux pommes flambéed with Calvados and fresh fish, such as this recipe baked with fresh herbs and vegetables. The simplicity of this dish lifts it high above many others that take hours in preparation.

In the Windward Islands one winter we were lucky enough to catch a red snapper as they are known there, big enough to feed both guests and crew and, although we struggled to fit such a large fish in the oven, having at the last resorted to removing tail and head, the meal was enjoyed by one and all.

1 large bream
½ glass olive oil
4 very beautiful ripe tomatoes
3 onions
2 cloves garlic
thyme, bay and parsley
2 glasses white wine
100g black olives
salt and pepper

For the stuffing:
3 tbsp olive oil
125g streaky bacon
2 onions
3 leaves of chard
a few salted fillets of anchovy
2 cloves of garlic
1 cup of the crumb of a loaf of white bread soaked in milk and then squeezed
plenty of chopped flat parsley

fishing boats n the Windward Islands

Prepare the stuffing. Wash the anchovy fillets to remove some of the salt. Chop the streaky bacon into small dice. Finely chop the onions and garlic.

Wash the green part of the chard leaves, dry and roll, and with the aid of a large knife chop them finely.

Cook the onions in the oil until they soften, add the bacon, cook for a couple of seconds, then add the chard leaves, anchovies and garlic. Mix all with a wooden spoon over a gentle heat, mashing the anchovy fillets. When the chard is soft add the 'mie' of bread and the chopped parsley. Taste carefully for seasoning.

Make sure the fish is scaled – in France, the fishmonger always does this awful task, but here I am not so sure.

Lay the fish on its stomach and break the central bone from the head to the tail and remove it. Alternatively, the fish can be filleted after cooking but it is agreeable if the majority of the bones are gone. Stuff the fish carefully and fold the 2 sides back together.

Oil a large oven dish. Finely chop the onions and soften them a little in the oil over a gentle heat, add the peeled and chopped tomatoes, the pressed garlic, the destoned olives and the herbs. Moisten this with the white wine and place the fish on top.

Cook in a hot oven for about 25 minutes. Serve straight from the oven in the cooking dish.

FLYING FISH PIE

I have to mention at this fishy stage in my book my flying fish pie.

Very often mid-Atlantic, when I emerged with my cup of morning tea or when I was lucky enough to be on the dawn watch, I would find the deck covered in these amazing little fish that fly along the crests of the waves catching the sun on their beautiful soft colours of skin and wings. How cruel it was for them to land and die on our decks, which a great many of them did. I found a West Indian recipe for flying fish pie but it was simply dreadful, these fish being full of a mass of tiny bones. One would have to be quite desperate to try to eat them!

flying fish

SNAPPER CREOLE

This was a recipe that I frequently made in the Caribbean, and it seemed to work very well for any small variety of white fish that anyone caught and presented me with to cook for dinner.

1.5kg of red snapper
seasoned flour
1 lemon

For the sauce:
1 large chopped onion
3 stalks celery, chopped
1 green pepper, chopped
60g butter
2 cloves
grated lemon rind
2 tbsp chopped parsley
½ tsp each of rosemary and thyme
1 bay leaf
2 cloves of finely chopped garlic
6 large ripe tomatoes
1 tbsp Worcester sauce
Tabasco
salt, black pepper and sugar

Rosemary

thyme

Gently cook the onion, celery and pepper in a frying pan with the butter, until soft. Add the cloves, lemon zest, herbs and garlic. Peel and chop the tomatoes, add to the mixture in the pan and cook for about 20–25 minutes until it becomes a thick purée. Stir in the Worcester sauce and seasonings.

Sprinkle the fish with flour and place in an oven-proof baking dish with the sauce poured around and between them. Arrange lemon slices on top and bake for 30–40 minutes.

NAGE DE SAINT-JACQUES CORAILLES

Scallops are big business off our Dorset coast and most good restaurants of merit have them on the menu somewhere whilst they are in season. This delicious recipe originates from Brittany; 'nager' means to swim or bathe so the scallops are bathed in their cooking juices with fresh herbs and tangy sorrel leaves. I love eating them but after many encounters, first in Guernsey where they have a small delicate variety 'Guernsey Queens' and later sailing around the Brittany coast and finally a disastrous meal in St Malo, I have come to terms with the fact that I am violently allergic to scallops.

16 good sized scallops, preferably with the roe or coral still attached
70g of butter
25cl dry white wine
2 chopped shallots
12 sorrel leaves
1 carrot, 1 leek, tarragon, chervil and salt and pepper

Clean the scallops, keeping the nut of flesh and the coral. Discard the black pouch and wash and dry each shellfish carefully.

Butter an oven dish and sprinkle with chopped shallots. Cut the flesh in thick slices across and place these with the coral on the shallots. Moisten with the white wine, cover with foil and cook for 7 or 8 minutes in a hot oven.

To prepare 'La Nage'

Cut the peeled leek and carrot in fine julienne strips and cook gently in butter for 2 minutes; add the cooking juices of the scallops and several tarragon leaves. Adjust the seasoning.

Butter individual oven dishes, line them with sorrel leaves and place in the oven for 2 minutes. Arrange the scallops in these dishes and scatter the juliennes of vegetables over the fish. Reduce the remaining cooking juices and add the butter to make a sauce. Pour this hot smooth mixture over the scallops and serve sprinkled with chervil.

LOUP AU FENOUIL

On Atlantic crossings the most prized fish for us to catch was a king fish, a beautiful fish not unlike a huge mackerel. The recipes for 'loup de mer' – quite literally, the wolves of the sea – were well-suited to this fish whenever we were lucky enough to catch some en route to the Antilles. Our translation for the wolf here is sea bass, and on my return to Dorset I found them to be a small fish here with none of the same majestic charm but still delicious, although the taste of farmed fish is disappointing and fresh wild sea bass are only available from August through to March.

The fennel, however, is always available here, and is grown locally in season. It complements beautifully the sweet flesh of this magnificent fish.

1 large sea bass of about 1½kg if possible, or individual fish suitable for one person
a bunch of fresh or dried fennel fronds
2 tsp fennel seeds
½ glass olive oil
salt and pepper
baking parchment in which to wrap your fish

For the sauce:
1 bowl of firm home-made mayonnaise made with
1tsp of Dijon mustard, 1 egg yolk and 25cl of oil
3 tbsp capers
3 gherkins
chopped parsley, chervil and tarragon

Scale and clean the fish and dry it well. Make several cuts along the skin on both sides and sprinkle with the fennel seeds. Place a branch of fennel inside.

Wrap the fish securely in baking paper sitting on fennel fronds and more of the same placed on the fish itself. Twist the ends of the parcel and place on a roasting grill in an oven dish. Place this in the middle of a moderately hot oven for 20–25 minutes.

Loup de Mer

While the fish is cooking, prepare the sauce, add the chopped capers and gherkins and all the chopped herbs to your bowl of firm mayonnaise.

Open the package on serving to your guests, as the aromas escaping are not to be missed, and serve the sauce alongside.

XIFIAS SOUVLAKIA – SWORDFISH ON SKEWERS

On our whistle-stop cruises of Greece with guests who believed that the next anchorage would always be better than the last, I fell in love with Greek markets, the essence and smell of them. Barrels of salty feta, bowls of thick yogurt, olives in abundance, piles of melon and trucks with whole tuna and swordfish, almost as big as the vehicle itself, being sliced and sold in chunks to eager customers. Domestica and retsina, the local wines, so resinous and ugly to a fine wine palate on first taste, but after a few weeks one becomes accustomed.

We took on a Greek deck hand and he taught me his mothers' secret recipes for tzatziki and taramasalata; and how to stuff vine leaves to perfection, oozing with the wonderful taste of the Greek pungent olive oil. The wasps were the only thing I could have lived without, and our crew arguing in the early morning about who would have to venture out to lift the anchor, as the enemy would appear in swarms from the pine trees as soon as I opened the fridge to prepare breakfast even though my galley was tightly sealed and air conditioned.

1kg swordfish, boned, skinned and cubed
salt and freshly ground black pepper
juice of 2 lemons strained
¼ cup olive oil
chopped fresh thyme
8 cherry tomatoes
8 bay leaves
2 green peppers, seeded and cubed

Season the cubed fish lightly with salt and pepper, and set aside.

Whisk together the lemon juice, oil and thyme, and place the swordfish in this marinade for a short while, before threading on wooden or metal sticks alternately with the peppers, bay leaves and tomatoes. Cook on the barbeque or under the grill for 15 minutes, turning frequently and brushing with the marinade.

Serve immediately.

thyme

we found a donkey marooned on an island in Greece

CRABES FARCI

The little freshwater land crabs used in this recipe I only ever came across in 2 places, one of course being Martinique, and the other Turkey where some cruising guests went on a river trip and brought them back proudly for supper. They nip horribly and hard, and can escape from a bucket in double-quick time. Nevertheless, they are delicious cooked in the Martiniquais way. I believe that their survival in the mangroves is now threatened by their popularity as a dish in the restaurants on the island.

The same recipe can of course be used with great success with the crabs that are caught off the Dorset coast.

6 small crabs
100g fresh breadcrumbs
1 finely-chopped, seeded red pepper
3 tbsp snipped chives
2 tbsp chopped parsley
2 cloves of garlic, crushed
1 tbsp lime juice
salt and freshly ground black pepper
¼ tsp allspice
3 tbsp dark rum, preferably from Martinique
butter

Plunge the crabs into boiling water and cook for 8–10minutes. Remove and cool. Carefully take the meat from the shells and claws and chop finely. Discard the spongy fibre and scrub the empty shells.

Mash 75g of the breadcrumbs into the crabmeat until the mixture is smooth. Add the hot pepper, chives, parsley, garlic, lime juice, seasoning, allspice and rum, mixing thoroughly. Stuff the shells with the prepared stuffing. If using large crabs use ramekin dishes or scallop shells.

Sprinkle with the remaining breadcrumbs, dot with butter and bake in a moderately hot oven for 30 minutes or until lightly brown. Serve as an appetizer or light lunch.

Les petites crabes de Martinique

TUNA COOKED THE MARTINIQUE WAY

When we sailed down islands to Martinique I could not wait for the treats that awaited us there; the glistening market full of fruit and vegetables and normal produce that I was used to having available for my galley in Europe, and of course with plenty of West Indian delicacies as well. I would store away as much as I possibly could to give my menus, whilst cruising the other islands, some flavour and sparkle. So it is only right to include a few of the recipes that I borrowed from restaurants there, as the local specialties were definitely the most memorable in the west Antilles.

8 tbsp lime juice
1 fresh red hot pepper ground
3 cloves of garlic
1 tbsp salt
350cl cold water
6 tuna steaks
flour
4 tbsp olive oil
1 finely chopped onion
4 chopped spring onions
2 medium tomatoes, peeled and chopped
salt and freshly ground black pepper
1 bay leaf and a ¼ tsp of thyme
1 tbsp olive oil

La Tortue aux isles de Cannes

In a large bowl mix together 6 tbsp of lime juice with the hot pepper, 2 of the cloves of garlic crushed, the salt and water. Soak the fish in this marinade, adding a little more water if needed to cover. After 1 hour dry the fish, discarding the liquid.

Dust the fish with flour and, using a heavy pan, sauté in the olive oil until golden. Keep the fish warm.

Add a little more oil to the pan and sauté the onion and spring onions until tender but not brown. Add the tomatoes, salt and pepper, bay leaf and thyme and cook for 5 minutes. Add the tuna and enough water to make sure the fish is covered, and cook for 10–15 minutes until the fish is tender. Discard the bay leaf and, just before serving, mix together the remaining clove of crushed garlic, 2 tbsp of lime juice and 1 tbsp olive oil, and pour over the fish.

SMOKED TROUT TART WITH HORSERADISH

Smoked trout is available from our wonderful smokery in Bridport and fresh horseradish is grown by our local green grocer in season, although I notice that for some it is quite a new ingredient, of which they are unaware, preferring to buy it in a jar. Freshly-grated horseradish is an experience definitely not to be missed if the opportunity arises. Simply peel the root and grate it like fresh ginger – it stores well in the fridge wrapped in film, but will go brown if left in the air.

600g puff pastry rolled out to about 3mm of thickness
5 smoked trout
2 tbsp grated horseradish
parsley, chervil and chives
egg yolk to glaze the tart
3 eggs
10ml crème frâiche
salt and pepper
a pinch of grated nutmeg

Line a tart tin approx 24cms diameter with two-thirds of the pastry. Fillet the trout or, if already filleted, check for bones.

Prick the base of the tart and lie half the trout fillets in the pastry case, spread with half the horseradish and half the chopped herbs. Make a second layer exactly like the first – fish, horseradish and herbs.

Roll out a cover for the tart and seal the edges with a little egg yolk.

Make a small round hole in the centre and place a chimney of rolled baking paper or foil to keep it open. Brush the tart with the remaining egg yolk.

Cook for 30 minutes in a moderately hot oven. Mix the egg yolks with the crème frâiche, salt and pepper and nutmeg. Pour this mixture down the little chimney and replace the dish in the oven for a further 15 minutes. Serve very hot.

SQUID WITH TOMATOES & WINE

We had an Egyptian girl with us for an extended cruise of the Greek islands and she used to dive off the rocks and come up a few moments later with huge octopus which she would then kill and proceed to tenderize on the rocks before she brought them back onboard for me to cook. Some say they taste like lobster, but I would say they lack a little something. Squid, however, is a better bet, easier to cook and much more tender.

1kg squid
1 large chopped onion
1 clove of garlic crushed
olive oil
500g tomatoes
1 tbsp tomato concentrate
1 glass of red wine
sugar, salt and black pepper
paprika
chopped parsley

When first faced with fresh squid I struggled, but I managed to work out which bits you ate and which bits to discard! If you pull the head from the body, you discover a piece of transparent bone inside the bag that can be pulled out and thrown away. Remove the purple skin from the sack and wash thoroughly. Cut into rings, including the side flaps. Take the tentacles from the head and chop them too. Keep the ink sac and throw away the head and soft entrails. It is a lot simpler than it sounds and by the time you have done a dozen for dinner, you will be an expert.

Dry the squid and fry in a little oil in a large saucepan with the onion and garlic. Add the tomatoes peeled and chopped, the concentrate and the wine. Season lightly. Crush the ink sacs, dilute with a little water and strain into the pan. Simmer for 25 minutes uncovered and then remove the squid to a warm serving dish.

Reduce the sauce to a pleasing consistency, adjusting the seasoning by adding salt, black pepper, sugar and paprika. When the sauce is rich and appetizing, pour over the squid pieces, sprinkle with chopped parsley and serve very hot.

VEGETABLE DISHES

La cocotte verte

Presentation, I noticed as soon as I stepped on French shores, where food is concerned, is nearly always effortless and perfect. That chic combination of the right food in the right dish never seems to escape the cook, and all manner of different shaped and sized oven-ready receptacles are always by his or her side. The average French housewife has an attention to detail that far surpasses her British counterpart, and I know I have learnt from this. I have a well-used and very well-travelled collection of tart tins that have clattered behind me as I have cooked around the islands of the Mediterranean and Caribbean, and now they nestle in a drawer at *Le Vieux Four*. If I have to throw one away it is like the departure of an old friend to be seriously mourned.

SPRING ONION & GINGER TART

A fresh tasting, spicy tart and a definite candidate for the long loose-bottomed tart dish you have been longing to use, the spring onions fitting well without too much of a trim

200g puff pastry
1 large bunch of spring onions
200g yogurt
60g freshly grated parmesan
1 piece of fresh ginger about 3 cm
cumin
black pepper
2 eggs
1 tbsp oil
butter for the dish
salt

Roll out the pastry quite thinly into a rectangle. If you can find a long removable bottom tart tin, this dish would suit it well, otherwise I have a square one that works too, fitting the length of the spring onions.

Butter and line with the pastry, cutting off the surplus around the edge. Press foil into the pastry, having pricked it with a fork, and bake it blind for 15 minutes.

Cut the roots and any damaged leaves off the spring onions and wash them. Peel the ginger, cut in very thin slices and cook for 5 minutes in a frying pan with the oil and several spoonfuls of water. When the water has taken the flavour of the ginger, add the spring onions and cook for 10 minutes. Strain and dry the onions and place them in the prepared tart case, having removed the foil.

Reduce the cooking liquor to 1 soup spoonful. In the bowl of a mixer place the ginger with its juice, the yogurt, eggs and parmesan. Sprinkle these ingredients with black pepper and cumin and mix into a smooth cream. Pour this over the spring onions.

Cook in a hot oven for 35–40 minutes, keeping a careful watch, and if the tart takes too much colour, place baking paper over whilst finishing the cooking time. Let the tart sit for 15 minutes before serving, or it is equally good cold.

PISSALADIERE

From this masterful street snack that adorns the French early morning markets my little savoury tartelettes were born. In France it is purchased wrapped roughly in a piece of grease-proof paper and its irresistible ooze of flavour demands that you devour it whilst you shop.

My little tartelettes, however, are usually eaten sitting at Le Vieux Four with a salad or taken home to eat in the garden for a summer lunch. My own recipes replace the thick bready dough beneath with a crisp pastry that tends to remain fresher longer for transportation, but here is the original as it is made on the back streets of Nice.

400g plain white bread dough (see Pastry and Dough section)
2 soup spoons of olive oil

For the topping:
5 tbsp olive oil
1kg onions
1 small clove of garlic
8 salted anchovies
small black olives from Nice

Wash the anchovies to remove some of the salt and soak them until ready to use. Peel and chop the onions and garlic. Cook the onions and garlic in the oil until soft but not brown stirring all the time.

Knead 2 spoonfuls of olive oil into the bread and form into a round about 2cms thick. Place on an oiled and lightly-floured baking tray, and prick to prevent the dough rising too much during cooking. Spread the onion mixture carefully, leaving only a small border.

Criss-cross with the anchovies and decorate with an olive in each space. Drizzle with oil and cook in a hot oven for 15–20 minutes.

TARTELETTES SALE *Le Vieux Four*

A mixture of these tartelettes will make a delightful, colourful and tasty lunch or supper.

500g pâte brisée (see Pastry and Dough section)

This amount of pastry will line about eighteen 4" tartelette tins of the fluted kind. Roll the dough fairly thinly, then prick and bake the cases blind to keep the pastry crisp.

Tartes Provençales

Slice ripe tomatoes and arrange in the pastry shells. Sprinkle with Herbs de Provence and drizzle with my standard dressing for salad (see Sauce section). Scatter a flavoursome grated cheese such as mature Cheddar over the tartelettes and top with chopped black olives. Bake until the cheese is sizzling and the tomatoes are soft, about 15 minutes in a moderately hot oven. Sprinkle generously with chopped fresh basil to serve.

Spinach and mozzarella

Steam the spinach with a little salt and drain thoroughly, squeezing out excess moisture. To one small bowl of spinach add 1 egg yolk, 2 tbsp of crème frâiche and 100g of grated mozzarella. Adjust the seasoning with plenty of freshly ground black pepper and salt and a little grated nutmeg. Generously fill 4 of the tartelette cases and bake in a moderate oven for 20 minutes until beginning to brown.

Onion and goat's cheese

Peel and thinly slice 3 medium onions and fry them gently in 2 tbsp of oil in a heavy sauce pan until very soft and starting to take a little colour. Add 1 egg yolk, salt and black pepper and 2 tbsp of double cream. Fill 4 of the tartelette cases and lie a thick slice of French goat's cheese (the kind available in a log shape) on the top of each. Bake in a moderately hot oven until the onion mixture is set and the cheese melting and brown. Sprinkle with freshly snipped chives.

Mushroom and stilton with fresh tarragon

Fry 300g of chopped field mushrooms in a little butter and oil until the juices run and they are soft. Add 100g of crumbled Stilton, 1 egg yolk and 2 tbsp of thick cream. Season with black pepper but no salt as the cheese is salty enough and stir in the roughly chopped tarragon, Fill 4 tartelette cases and bake for 20mins in a moderately hot oven until the mushroom mixture is set.

estragon

Red onion and grape

Peel and chop 6 small red onions. Cook them over a moderate in ½ a glass of water that will evaporate. Sprinkle the onions with sugar and, turning up the heat, allow them to caramelize. Wash 8 red grapes and 8 black ones, both the seedless variety. Halve them unless they are small and add them to the onions along with a glass of white wine and a tbsp of white wine vinegar. Cook quickly until the liquid reduces to syrup and add 2 tbsp of double cream and a squeeze of lemon juice. Adjust the seasoning with salt and black pepper fill 4 tartelette cases and warm to serve.

Small sweet pepper and orange

This filling is best made with sweet peppers from the West Indies (Antillaise) or the long Romero peppers seeded and cut into chunks. Locally we have some small, sweet red peppers in the summer that are ideal. Wash and deseed 200g of peppers – if using the small ones simply halve them. Peel and chop 2 small onions and put in a frying pan with 4 tbsp of water and one of oil. Cover and cook for 10 minutes then turn up the heat and evaporate the juice. Add salt and pepper and a little powdered pimento. Mix 200ml thick cream with the zest and juice of ½ an orange and 1 egg yolk. Place the peppers in 4 pastry cases and pour over the cream mix seasoned with salt and a little pimento powder. Scatter with chopped spring onion and bake in a moderately hot oven for 20 minutes. Serve warm.

Remove the shells from the metal tins before baking with the fillings to avoid the tartelettes from sticking to the tins. Instead of making small tartelettte of course the mixtures could be used in the same way to fill a larger pastry case if desired.

COURGETTES A LA PROVENCALE

I have decided to include 2 courgette recipes as they are one vegetable I have managed to grow fairly easily in my Dorset garden, so I am sure a lot of others do too. I plant them in the spring when the frosts have passed and eagerly await the flowers and courgettes themselves. They are a much-underrated vegetable, too often overcooked and left devoid of texture and flavour, when they can be deliciously nutty and crisp. I often just cut them in half long-ways, sprinkle with herbs, brush with oil and put them on the barbeque, to accompany the meats grilling there.

This recipe makes a simple supper or lunch with perhaps some garlic bread.

1kg small courgettes
1 glass olive oil
1kg ripe soft tomatoes
2 onions
½ tsp sugar
2 cloves of garlic
parsley, thyme, bay and a branch of basil
40g grated Parmesan
salt and pepper

Wash but do not peel the courgettes, cut into lengths of about 2" and cut length ways in two. Blanche for 5 minutes in boiling salted water and then strain. Peel the tomatoes, take out the seeds and chop roughly pressing them to remove excess moisture. Peel and crush the garlic. Peel and chop the onions and gently fry them in 2 tbsp of oil until they begin to take colour. Sprinkle with the sugar, mix and add the tomatoes, herbs, garlic and seasonings. Let the sauce cook gently until thick.

Heat the rest of the oil in a frying pan and fry the courgettes until golden on each side. Arrange them in an oven dish. Strain the sauce and pour over, sprinkle with Parmesan and grill to serve.

BEIGNETS DES FLEURS DE COURGE

20 very fresh courgette flowers

For the batter:
1 egg and 1 yolk
1 tbsp olive oil
1 glass warm water
oil for frying
finely chopped parsley

Mix the batter 2 hours before use. Sieve the flour into a bowl, break the whole egg and put the white to one side. Put the 2 yolks into the centre of the flour with the spoonful of oil and mix with the water to make a thick, smooth batter adding the water carefully as it must not be too liquid. Leave to rest for 2 hours.

Prepare the courgette flowers leaving just the petals; wash and dry them carefully on adsorbent paper.

When you are ready to cook the flowers, fold the stiffly-beaten white of egg carefully into the batter. Heat the oil to fry the flowers, dip them in the batter and fry until golden. Serve on a folded serviette scattered with chopped parsley.

Les fleurs des courges

TARTE AUX ARTICHAUTS

For this tasty tart I use the artichoke hearts that one can buy in olive oil in a jar although you can make it with fresh, using just the base of the artichoke after having removed the leaves. I always had a few jars in my store cupboard at sea, and so was able to make this tart for lunch for my guests when far from shops and fresh produce and it never failed to impress.

300g pâte brisée (see Pastry and Dough section)
1 bottle of artichoke hearts in oil
40g butter
1 tbsp flour
2 ladles of milk
1 egg
1 tbsp crème frâiche
60g Parmesan
1 tbsp chopped parsley with garlic
salt and pepper
grated nutmeg

Drain the artichokes well.

Prepare a béchamel with the butter, flour and milk. Away from the heat add the egg, crème frâiche and the parmesan. Season and add the nutmeg and the parsley and garlic mix.

Roll out the pastry and line a tart dish for 4–6 people. Bake blind for 10 minutes.

Place the artichokes cut in half into the tart shell and cover with the sauce.

Cook for 35 minutes in a hot oven.

SOUFFLED VEGETABLE MOUSSE

A wonderful standby when vegetables were in short supply and I had to use my store of blanched vegetables in the freezer, either as a stand-alone lunch, in small ramekins as an appetizer, or to accompany a hearty meat dish.

Mousse Au Chou-Fleur

1 medium sized cauliflower
10cl crème frâiche
grated nutmeg
4 eggs
10g butter
½ red pepper and ½ green pepper to decorate
salt and pepper

Cut the cauliflower into florets and steam until soft. Mix to a purée in a food processor. Add the egg yolks and seasonings. Whip the whites until firm peaks are attained and fold carefully into the cauliflower purée.

Butter the inside of your chosen oven dish and bake for 40 minutes in a moderately hot oven. Turn the mousse out on to a warm serving dish and decorate with strips of grilled peppers.

This dish could be made with broccoli, carrots, artichoke bases or potatoes.

FENOUIL EN CROUTE

La Marmite

I have borrowed this recipe from a restaurant in a small back street of Antibes, called 'La Marmite', with a black sign hanging outside in the shape of a traditional marmite. To my joy some friends of mine went there recently and found it still there some 25 years on, but I am sure the original owners and chefs have long since moved.

4 small fennel bulbs

180g small mushrooms

60g shallots

100g fromage blanc

1 tsp sunflower oil

1 tbsp chopped parsley

salt

For the pastry:

150g flour

80g margarine

2 eggs

salt

Cut the fennel bulbs in half lengthways and cook in boiling salted water for 15 minutes. Strain them well.

Prepare the pastry, mixing the margarine cut into small pieces, and a whole egg with the salt, quickly and lightly into the flour with the tips of your fingers. Squeeze together into a ball and leave to rest in the fridge.

Heat the oil in a saucepan and cook the finely-chopped shallots and mushrooms over a gentle heat until all the moisture has evaporated.

Take off the heat and add the fromage blanc, the parsley and some salt. Garnish the inside of each fennel bulb with this mixture.

Roll the pastry out thinly into 8 rectangles approx 12 x 8 cm and place a piece of fennel on each, with the stuffing side against the pastry. Wrap them carefully, joining and glazing with the beaten egg. Cook for 30 minutes in a moderately hot oven until golden, and serve immediately.

POIS CHICHES AUX HERBES

In the back streets of Nice the North African influence is very noticeable in the restaurants and markets. Chick peas and chick pea flour often feature in Algerian cooking. Traditionally, it is baked until blistered and brown in a wood fired oven. Couscous restaurants abound here too, interspersed with very good pizzas as the Italian influence is also strong.

500g chickpeas in a tin
2 tomatoes
1 glass white wine
1 onion
1 clove of garlic
1 tbsp chopped rosemary
1 tbsp chopped basil
some small sage leaves
a few sprigs of dill
2 tbsp olive oil
salt and pepper

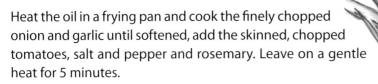

Heat the oil in a frying pan and cook the finely chopped onion and garlic until softened, add the skinned, chopped tomatoes, salt and pepper and rosemary. Leave on a gentle heat for 5 minutes.

Rinse and strain the chickpeas.

Tip the wine and chickpeas in with the onion tomato mixture and ½ the sage leaves. Cover and cook gently for a further 30 minutes.

Pour the chickpeas and their sauce into a serving dish and scatter with basil, dill and the rest of the sage leaves to serve.

SOCCA

Huge wide trays of Socca are seen on street corners outside small restaurants, the dish being a kind of pancake cooked in a large round copper pan and then cut and folded into portions and sold wrapped in a paper cone.

300g chickpea flour

500ml water

2 tbsp olive oil

1 tsp salt

pepper

cumin for a smoky woody flavour

Mix the ingredients to a batter that should be slightly thinner than pancake mix and smooth with no lumps. Pour a little oil into a metal skillet and heat it in the oven before pouring in enough of the batter to cover the bottom in a thin layer, and replace into the oven until bubbling and brown. A non-stick tart tin can also work quite well.

Serve hot as a nibble with pre-dinner drinks.

Socca de Nice

GRATIN AUX TROIS LEGUMES

One of my favourite vegetable dishes to accompany a roast or just to have for a light lunch or simple supper.

100g grated Emmental
3 carrots
6 leeks, only the white part
grated nutmeg
1 egg
50g butter
20cl milk
1 tbsp chopped flat parsley or coriander
500g potatoes
salt and pepper

Peel and slice the potatoes thinly and bring to the boil in salted water for 5 minutes or until beginning to soften. Rinse in cold water, strain and leave to cool.

Cut the leeks into fine rounds. Peel the carrots and grate them. Heat 30g of butter in a frying pan and cook the leeks for 6–8 minutes over a gentle heat, stirring frequently. Cook the carrots in boiling salted water for 1 minute and drain thoroughly.

In a bowl, mix together the milk with the egg, a little grated nutmeg, half the Emmental cheese and the seasonings.

In a buttered oven dish, layer the potatoes, followed by the leeks and finally, the carrots. Pour over the cheese mixture and sprinkle with the rest of the cheese and dots of butter. Cook for 20–25 minutes in a moderately hot oven and serve in the oven dish.

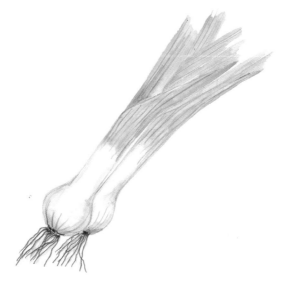

COLUMBO DE GIAUMON

Pumpkin is a very important vegetable in the West Indies and Bermuda for both sweet and savoury dishes. This curry is easy and tasty and can be served as a main dish with rice or with meat or poultry.

2 tbsp vegetable oil
30g unsalted butter
100g bacon
1 medium onion
1 bell pepper, seeded and chopped
1 tsp curry powder
¼ tsp ground cloves
2 medium tomatoes peeled and chopped
500g pumpkin, peeled and cut into 1" cubes
salt and freshly ground black pepper
1 large clove of garlic, crushed

Heat the oil and butter in a heavy saucepan, add the bacon, onion and pepper, and cook, stirring from time to time, until the onion and pepper are soft but not brown. Add the curry powder and cook for a minute or two, followed by the cloves, tomatoes, pumpkin and seasonings. Stir to mix and cook on a very low heat, covered and stir from time to time to prevent burning. When the pumpkin is very soft almost a purée, stir in the garlic and cook uncovered for a minute or so.

ACRATS DE CHOU PALMISTE

Hearts of palm were another standby tin always to be found in my store cupboard aboard ship and another cook in the islands showed me how to make these little spicy fritters to eat with drinks or as part of a lunchtime menu. The recipe originates from Martinique, as do many of the tastiest recipes in the islands.

For 6 people:
500g tin palm hearts, drained and coarsely chopped
225g flour
1 tsp baking powder
1 tsp salt
2 eggs, lightly beaten
1 medium onion, finely chopped
1 minced clove of garlic
2 fresh hot red or green peppers, finely chopped
1 tbsp chopped parsley
½ tsp thyme
salt and freshly ground black pepper to taste
3 tbsp milk if needed
oil to fry

thyme

Sift together into a bowl the flour, baking powder and salt. Stir in the eggs, onions, garlic, peppers, thyme, pepper and the palm hearts, folding the ingredients lightly to form a stiffish dough. Add some milk if necessary.

Stand the batter for 1 hour and then fry in a tablespoon of hot oil until golden brown. This can be done in a deep fryer but I always managed perfectly well in a frying pan as long as the oil is hot. Drain on paper towel and serve hot.

MEAT AND POULTRY DISHES

au travaille

Just a few of my favourite dishes, recipes picked up a long the way and used frequently at sea and now finally at home here in Dorset.

The Aga is, of course, a wonderful tool for cooking meat slowly over time, but my gas oven sets low as well and achieves the same result.

Some of the best meals I have ever eaten have been on Sunday jaunts in Provence to small roadside restaurants to eat their menu of the day – often blissfully simple but outstandingly good. Maybe just a dish of radishes and baguette and butter to start, followed by a steaming plate of daube with perhaps some garlicky beans, and to finish a glazed tart aux pommes and a slice of smelly local goat's cheese. Perfection!

My first task when I joined the American vessel in Fort Lauderdale was to prepare dishes for the freezer for our trip to Europe, so I busied myself making varied meat dishes to feed both guests and crew. We set out and one of the main engines failed and so we ended up in Bermuda for a few months but the meals were tasty all the same, even though we were tied to the quay. They have the biggest cockroaches in Bermuda I have ever seen and they would try to board at night so we would have to move a little away from the quay on long ropes!

DAUBE PROVENCALE

This is the most traditional stew from Provence cooked by French housewives through the generations. The dish tastes even better as it is reheated over a few days and the leftovers would be used to make a filling for cannelloni, ravioli or other pasta dishes.

Use about 1.5kg of good stewing beef for 6 people and ask the butcher to cut it into pieces of about 100g

225g streaky bacon
2 tbsp olive oil
2 carrots
3 onions
4 large ripe tomatoes
5 cloves of garlic
1 piece orange zest
1 tsp sugar
salt and black pepper

For the marinade:
2 onions
1 carrot
bouquet garni of fresh herbs, thyme, bay, rosemary, parsley stalks and celery leaves
enough good red wine to cover the meat
3 tbsp wine vinegar

Romarin

Prepare the marinade: peel and chop the onions and the carrot; put them into a bowl with the herbs, and the pieces of beef. Season and pour in the wine and vinegar. Leave to marinate for a few hours.

When the meat is ready, peel and chop the onions and carrots and dry the chunks of beef. Peel the tomatoes and take out the seeds. Chop and press the pulp to extract excess liquid. Crush the garlic.

Take the herbs from the marinade and put to one side. Reduce the marinade by half over a gentle heat.

Chop the bacon and cook in a large pan over a gentle heat until the grease runs. Take out the morsels of bacon, and in the remaining fat fry the onions, carrots and beef until brown. Add the tomato pulp, the garlic and the herbs, and finally, the reduced marinade, topping up with a little bouillon if the beef is not covered. Add the sugar and bring to a simmer.

Tip into a large ovenproof dish adding the orange peel and place covered in a moderately hot oven for 1 hour and then lower the temperature for at least 2 hours. If the daube can be cooked for a further 2 hours at a slow temperature the following day it will improve significantly.

2 anchovy fillets that have been desalted by soaking in a little milk are traditionally mixed with a small crushed garlic clove and a few drops of olive oil and added the sauce at the end of cooking time.

BOEUF EN MARINADE

This recipe makes a wonderful tender piece of meat with an outstanding sauce, without being too complicated.

1½kg sirloin
4 large onions
1 branch of thyme
3 bay leaves
10 grains black pepper
½ glass white wine vinegar
100g bacon
70g crème frâiche
¼ tsp flour
40g butter

Peel the onions and cook them in thick rounds. Place the roast in a bowl and cover with the onion rounds. Add the thyme, bay and pepper and sprinkle with the vinegar and 2 glasses of cold water. Leave to marinate for 24 hours and turn the meat from time to time.

After the marination dry the meat and cut the bacon in dice. In an oven dish, fry the bacon dice in the butter for 3 minutes and then brown the meat on all sides. Salt the meat at this point.

Pour the marinade into a saucepan and bring to the boil. Let the meat cook for 30 minutes uncovered in a moderately hot oven and baste frequently with the hot marinade to prevent the roast from drying.

Five minutes before the end of the cooking time, place the flour in a bowl and dilute with the crème frâiche, mixing well. Pour this in to the pot with the meat and mix with the roasting juices. Allow this to cook gently for 5 minutes and then serve the roast with the hot sauce alongside.

CARBONADES DE BOEUF A LA FLAMANDES

*All the crews I ever worked with drank lager, Heineken, Michelob, San Miguel, Stella Artois –
wherever we were, there was always a favorite. Sometimes I would manage to steal some to
cook this recipe and though I was always told it was a waste of a good beer, I would always
disagree.*

1½kg lean beef for braising, cut into slices about 1cm thick
750g onions
1 bouquet garni
3 tbsp margarine
2 cloves
1 small piece of cinnamon
1 litre lager
1 cup bouillon
1 tbsp dark brown sugar
1 tbsp Dijon mustard
2 large thin slices of stale pain de campagne, or similar heavy bread
salt and freshly ground black pepper

Peel and chop the onions. Heat the margarine and quickly seal the slices of beef. Drain
and set to one side. In the same pan, soften the onions.

Heat the oven quite hot, dry the slices of bread and spread with the mustard.

In an ovenproof dish or terrine, layer the beef and onions alternately, seasoning each
layer. Place in the centre the cinnamon, herbs and cloves; moisten with the beer and
bouillon, sprinkle with the brown sugar and lay the slices of bread to finish. Cover the
dish and cook in a moderately hot oven for 30 minutes, then lower the heat to a slow
temperature and cook for a further 2 hours.

To serve, drain the beef slices and the onions and transfer them to a hot dish. Remove
the cinnamon and herbs and break down the slices of bread to thicken the juice, pour
over the meat and serve very hot.

Something smells so good

GNOCCHI A LA ROMAINE

Here I shall add, amongst the recipes for rustic meat dishes, how to make gnocchi. Originating from Nice, this recipe shows the strong Italian influence on the region. It is the perfect dish to accompany the stews, daubes and pot roasts in this section.

½ litre milk
125g semolina
100g grated cheese
salt, pepper and nutmeg
1tbsp marjoram and chives, or chopped spring onions
butter
1 egg

Bring the milk to the boil in a double saucepan, with salt, pepper, nutmeg, marjoram and chives. When the milk boils put the semolina in and stir until the mixture has the consistency of porridge. Take off the heat and stir in the beaten egg, 30g of cheese and 30g of butter. Pour into a buttered tin and spread to ½ cm thickness. Leave to cool.

Cut into rounds the size of a 10p piece and arrange in buttered gratin dish, putting more butter and the rest of the cheese on the top. Heat under the grill or in a hot oven until the gnocchi are brown. A little of the sauce from the meat poured over the gnocchi is delicious.

NAVARIN OF LAMB

Just the best navarin of lamb I have ever made, based on an old French recipe, of course. It loses none of its charm if frozen and produced mid-Atlantic in steaming bowls with garlic bread.

1.75kg shoulder of lamb, boned and cut into pieces
½ glass oil
50g butter
½ litre water or stock
20 small onions, peeled
12 small carrots
8 small long turnips
150g petit pois
150g green beans
1 medium onion with 2 cloves pressed in
2 sprigs rosemary
2 sprigs summer savory or sage
1 tbsp flour
salt and pepper

Romarin

In a heavy oven proof dish, heat the oil and butter and brown the onions and meat. When everything is golden, sprinkle with the flour and continue to cook, stirring until the flour browns. Add the water or stock, the onion with the cloves, the herbs and seasonings and bring to the boil.

Peel the carrots and turnips and add to the dish. Blanche the green beans for 5 minutes in boiling salted water and add them with the petit pois to the meat. Cover and cook in a moderate oven for 1½ hours. Sprinkle with fines herbes on serving.

Sea W tch

COUSCOUS

Too many of my friends say 'oh no, I don't like couscous', but have they ever wandered the back streets of Nice and eaten this dish as it should be? I doubt it. A traditional North African dish, it really can be very good.

1kg shoulder of mouton cut into chunks
500g turnips
1 glass oil
2 large onions, chopped finely
2 carrots, chopped in batons
1 tomato, peeled and cut in 4
1 tsp allspice
1 tsp powdered sweet red pepper
1 pinch coriander
1 minced hot red pepper
1 large tin chickpeas

In a big oven dish heat the oil and brown the turnips. Put them to one side and brown the lamb pieces. Add the onions, carrots and tomato and replace the turnips. Sprinkle in the spices and peppers, followed by the rinsed chickpeas. Moisten with 1 litre of water. Cover, bring to the boil and then cook in a slow oven or over a small flame for 1½ hours minimum.

For the grain:
Couscous grain is available prepared nowadays so it is very quick and easy to cook
1½ cups couscous
2¾ cups water or chicken stock, which gives it a delicious flavour

Bring the water or stock to the boil with a little salt. Off the heat, add the couscous grain and leave to rest for 5 minutes until the all the water is absorbed. The couscous should be fluffy, not gummy.

La tagine

ROAST LAMB WITH ORANGE & ROSEMARY SAUCE

When I studied for my cookery diploma in London all those years ago I compiled a big file of recipes I liked and this has travelled with me everywhere I have cooked. Some sheets are typed, others hand written and barely legible, and most are stained with sauces and drips from the kitchen. This file is one of the most precious things I own – the recipes inside not flamboyant or exciting, just simple, tasty and memorable.

1 large leg of lamb

For the glaze:
1 tbsp French mustard
1 tbsp bitter marmalade
juice of one orange
1 tbsp of dark brown sugar

Insert some slivers of garlic into the meat and 2 or 3 sprigs of rosemary. Roast the joint, and half an hour before the end of the cooking time, remove the skin and then glaze the meat.

Skim the fat off the juices in the pan and make a sauce by adding white wine, orange juice and Madeira or Marsala, making sure the sauce is piquant and not too sweet. Segment 2 oranges and, heating them through carefully in the sauce, serve them around the joint. Pour some sauce over the joint and serve the rest separately in a sauceboat.

POULET A L'AIGRE-DOUX

A tangy recipe, quick to do and liked by all.

6 chicken breasts, flattened out to allow a quick cooking time
20ml cider vinegar
2 tbsp Dijon mustard
2 tbsp soy sauce
2 tbsp honey
1 tsp thyme leaves, carefully destalked
10 basil leaves, finely chopped
salt and freshly ground black pepper

In a bowl, place the vinegar, mustard, soy sauce, honey, thyme, half of the basil and a little salt and plenty of ground black pepper. Mix well and add the chicken breasts, then leave to marinate for 20 minutes in the fridge.

Dry the chicken, and grill or shallow fry until cooked and golden, turning them so they are well browned. During this time, tip the marinade into a small pan and bring to a gentle boil for 4 or 5 minutes to reduce.

Serve the hot chicken drizzled with the marinade and sprinkled with the rest of the basil.

POLLO AL AJILLO

Le Monsieur

The chickens throughout the book are all in my kitchen and they each have a story of their own. As I have never been one for collecting dysfunctional china, they have all been gifted to me at some stage along the way. The two that spring to mind are the fat hen and her cockerel mate. My mother and stepfather became small holders in Dorset some forty or so years ago, running a few Dartmoor sheep and a couple of cows. All of these were known personally by name and I found it sad when they went inevitably into the deep freeze.

They sent their last poor old cow to the abattoir and the same day my stepfather had a very ill-timed heart attack, and as I had just returned for a few days from Spain I was allocated the task of butchering the cow, Daisy as she was commonly known. She had been fed on lush grass and most of this seemed to have turned into solid fat and the whole kitchen was knee deep in this for a couple of days. The bits that my stepfather deemed as edible from his presiding seat in a wheelchair by the door were so tough that any self respecting dog would have had trouble to chew and digest them.

I plodded on labeling and chopping on what turned out to be the worst culinary adventure of my life, I would say. A couple of days afterwards, my mother presented me with the two aforementioned Spanish china chickens as a thank-you and, I fear, as a constant reminder of this terrible task.

This recipe I collected in Spain, Estepona to be exact, where there used to be a little restaurant that made this dish to perfection. The garlic baked unpeeled becomes soft and sweet and imparts its flavour through the whole bird.

40 cloves of garlic
1 chicken, of about 1.8kg cut into joints
1 small glass Spanish cognac
1 glass dry white wine
80g butter
salt and pepper

La Madame

Heat the butter in an oven dish until sizzling, and brown the chicken pieces for 10 or 12 minutes. Add the unpeeled cloves of garlic and salt and pepper, continue to cook for 5 more minutes.

Add the cognac and flame quickly, leave for 10 minutes and then add the white wine. Cover the pot and place in a moderate oven for 40 minutes. Serve with the melting garlic cloves and pour the cooking juices over the chicken pieces.

POULET ANTIBOISE

Provencal chicken has become such a hackneyed dish on many restaurant menus and often bears little or no resemblance to this authentic dish. When carefully prepared with those succulent small, green olives from the south of France, which you can now find in jars here if you search the olives shelves in the supermarket or deli, it truly is a feast.

1 chicken of about 1.8kg, cut into pieces
½ litre olive oil + 8 tbsp
4 tbsp flour
2 lemons
1 tbsp vinegar
4 tomatoes, cut into 4
2 onions
150g green olives
1 clove of garlic
chopped parsley
2 branches tarragon
salt and pepper

estragon

Prepare a marinade with the lemon juice, 1 tbsp of vinegar, 6 tbsp of olive oil, 1tbsp chopped parsley, 2 onions cut in rounds, and salt and pepper. Place the chicken into this marinade for about an hour. Take the chicken and dry carefully before dipping in 4 tbsp of flour.

In a large deep frying pan, heat the ½ litre of olive oil and fry the chicken until golden over a fast flame. Reduce the heat and add the tomatoes and crushed garlic. Cook for about 40 minutes. Remove the pieces of chicken and serve on hot dish with the olives, tomatoes and garlic.

Make a sauce with the oil, lemon juice, chopped tarragon and some finely-chopped garlic. Adjust the seasoning and serve with the chicken.

the blue chicken

POLLO CON PINA A LA ANTIGUA

Before I first sailed into English Harbour in Antigua, I had been told about Mount Gay rum, the golden nectar made from the sugar cane in the islands. 'No, no' I protested 'I don't like any spirits'. Within days I was converted – not only drinking it mixed with sweetened coconut and fresh pineapple, but cooking with it too. The combination of the rum, the juices of the fruits of the islands and the spices to mix in or sprinkle on the top, never mind the sunshine, predictable winds and steel bands –I was in heaven.

juice and grated rind of one large lime
1.5kg chicken
salt and freshly ground pepper to taste
3 tbsp olive oil
1 medium onion, chopped
1 clove of garlic, chopped
2 ripe tomatoes, peeled and chopped
3 tbsp raisins
1 fresh hot red pepper, peeled and chopped
¼ tsp oregano
1 bay leaf
¼ pint rich chicken stock
350g coarsely-chopped fresh pineapple and juice
4 tbsp Mount Gay rum

Rub the lime juice and rind into the chicken pieces, season with salt and pepper and let stand for half an hour.

Heat the oil in a frying pan and sauté the chicken pieces until they take colour. Transfer the meat into a heavy oven dish. Sauté the onions in the frying pan until tender, add the tomatoes, raisins, hot pepper, oregano and bay leaf and cook, stirring for 5 minutes.

Pour over the chicken and add enough of the stock to almost cover the chicken. Cover and cook for about 45 minutes over a low heat until the chicken is tender.

Put the pineapple and juice into a small saucepan and cook until reduced by half. Add the rum, mix well and cook for a minute before pouring over the chicken to serve.

Les mangues de Martinque

CIVET DE LAPIN A LA FARIGOULETTE

Having saved enough money whilst cooking abroad, I did not do the sensible thing that most would choose and buy bricks and mortar. I bought a boat; a small wooden boat called Galuette, the name of a small seagull. This became my home and my dearest possession, with hours spent painting and varnishing to make her look just perfect. Short cruises were always on a tight budget and much rabbit was eaten! This recipe flavoured with thyme became a favourite, as was cruising the coast of Corsica, where the smell of thyme wafts out to sea on the breeze, as it grows wild along the cliff tops. I once was sailing here and glancing at the water beside Galuette, I noticed to my horror what appeared to be a green and brown island rising from the sea inches from my cockpit seat. Terrified, I rushed below and donned a life jacket for the first time in my life! Of course it was a whale, bigger than my boat and capable of sinking me without trace, should it choose to surface again. I called Monaco radio to tell them and give my position and they found the whole situation absolutely hilarious and I think, to this day, they quite doubted my sanity.

Galuette

1.5kg rabbit, jointed
1 litre red wine
2 stalks thyme for the marinade
3 stalks thyme, using just the leaves
2 bay leaves
a little chopped tarragon
2 tbsp flour
30g chopped bacon
18 small onions
6 shallots
3 cloves of garlic chopped
1 tbsp cognac
salt and pepper

thyme

Marinate the rabbit overnight in the red wine, perfumed with the stalks of thyme and bay leaves.

Next day, take the rabbit joints from the marinade and dry. Fry the bacon in a little oil in an oven dish. Take out and put to one side, dip the rabbit joints in flour and fry in the same oil. Add the onions, shallots and garlic. Let them cook together, stirring well, then add the cognac and replace the bacon.

Add half a litre of the marinade, heated through. Add the chopped thyme and tarragon, and season to taste. Cook over a gentle heat for 1½ hours.

PHEASANT WITH STILTON SAUCE
(or Roquefort works well too)

Living as I do now in this very gamey part of the world, it would be a shame not to include a few recipes for pheasant. I always seem to have at least a couple in the freezer, gifted kindly by my shooting friends, although I am not hugely keen on the sport, feeling that the pheasant does not really have a fair chance! However I appreciate that is a valued and much-enjoyed tradition, which also brings revenue to the West Country.

6 breasts of pheasant
100g butter
½ litre of white wine
200g mushrooms
salt and freshly ground black pepper

For the sauce:
60g flour
60g butter
¾ litre milk
200g Stilton
1 tbsp crème frâiche
salt and pepper

Brown the breasts in 50g of butter and let them cook through, slowly moistening with the wine as they cook. Sauté the mushrooms in the rest of the butter for 5 minutes and then add to the pheasant.

Make a béchamel sauce with the butter, flour and milk. Mash the cheese with the crème frâiche and add this to the sauce. Season carefully as the cheese is quite salty. When the pheasant is cooked, place the pieces and the mushrooms on a hot serving dish and cover with the stilton sauce.

FAISAN AUX RAISINS

Not dissimilar to pork and prunes, or duck with orange, pheasant and raisins make a good combination.

2 pheasants
200g raisins
250ml grape juice
100g crème frâiche
1 liqueur glass cognac
50g butter
salt and pepper

soak the raisins for 1 hour in the juice

Melt the butter in an oven dish and brown the pheasants on all sides. Drizzle with the cognac and flame. Moisten with the grape juice and cook for 1 hour on a gentle heat or slow oven.

Ten minutes before the end of cooking time, add the crème frâiche and soaked raisins. Taste and season the sauce before serving.

PHEASANT WITH LENTILS

This recipe uses the green lentils from Puy in France that apparently have the most nutritional value of all the lentil family.

2 pheasants
300g smoked bacon
2 onions
2 carrots
2 cloves
2 tbsp margarine
20cl chicken stock
2 thyme sprigs, 2 bay leaf, and 2 rosemary sprigs
400g green Puy lentils
2 cloves of garlic
salt and pepper

Romarin

Place the lentils in a sieve and rinse very thoroughly under the cold tap.

Season the clean and prepared birds inside and out. Cut the bacon into small pieces; chop one of the onions finely and pierce the other with the cloves. Peel the carrots, chop one finely and cut the other into small batons.

Melt the margarine in a deep oven dish and place the pheasants into the hot pan, surrounding them with the minced onion, carrot and bacon pieces. Stir over a brisk heat to brown all these ingredients on all sides. When they are a good colour, moisten with the bouillon, add half of the herbs, cover the dish and cook in moderate to slow oven for 1½ hours.

While the pheasants are cooking, place the lentils in a big saucepan with the peeled garlic. Cover with cold water, bring to a simmer and skim off the foam. Add the rest of the herbs, the onion pierced with cloves and the second carrot, and leave simmering for about an hour. Partially strain the lentils leaving them in a little of the cooking juice and spoon them around the pheasants. Season and replace in the oven for a further 30 minutes.

Serve the pheasants on a hot dish surrounded by the lentils, having removed the onion with cloves and the herbs.

JUST A FEW SAUCES ...

grann és double bóiles

My dear father always telephones me for instructions on hollandaise when his asparagus is ready in the garden because he says I have a foolproof method. I very rarely make complicated sauces and always look for the easy route to the best end. I turn the French method with Béarnaise and Hollandaise upside down and add the egg yolks to the hot butter instead of the other way around, and with this switch it never ever curdles or misbehaves. I have a small double boiler that belonged to my grandmother that is just perfect for the job.

SAUCE BEARNAISE

1 glass white wine vinegar
1 branch fresh tarragon
2 finely chopped shallots
3 egg yolks
200g of butter

estragon

Place the chopped shallots and vinegar in a small saucepan and over a gentle heat, reduce to one tbsp. Strain into the top of a small double boiler, discarding the shallots. Add the butter in pieces, placing over simmering water in the bottom half of the boiler, to melt.

Whisk the egg yolks with a fork and add them in a slow stream to the vinegar/butter mix, stirring all the time with a wooden spoon. As soon as the mixture starts to thicken, take the pan off the heat and stir for a couple more seconds until rich and creamy. Add salt to taste and chopped fresh tarragon. Pour into a sauce dish or bowl and serve warm with steak or chicken.

SAUCE HOLLANDAISE

2 egg yolks
150g butter
1 tsp of cold water
½ tsp salt

Melt the butter with the water in the top of a double boiler over simmering water. Whisk up the egg yolks with a fork and add in a steady stream to the hot butter, stirring with a wooden spoon to make a creamy sauce. Add salt to taste and serve warm with asparagus.

Delicious, too, with a squeeze of lemon to serve with grilled or oven-baked fish.

MAYONNAISE

It is so rare now that I see people make mayonnaise, as most prefer to take it from a jar, but homemade is a different beast and well worth the effort. The memory of fresh seafood platters in Brittany with huge bowls of mayonnaise freshly mixed, can never be replaced by a factory-produced substitute.

Take 1 egg yolk and mix with ½ tsp of Dijon mustard in a small bowl. Whisking continuously with a fork or small whisk, add olive or sunflower oil in preference to your taste or menu. When the sauce becomes too thick add a little vinegar or lemon juice to thin. One egg yolk will adsorb 1 cup of oil. Season to taste. This can be successfully done in a food processor or blender as long as the oil is always added slowly.

Poor Man's Mayonnaise is the same mix but without the egg, and is wonderful with avocado pears. The oil still thickens even without the presence of the egg yolk to give a sharp sauce that complements the blandness of the pear.

MAYONNAISE VERTE

1½ cups mayonnaise
8–10 spinach leaves
3–4 sprigs watercress
2 sorrel leaves
1 tbsp fresh tarragon
2 tbsp chopped spring onion

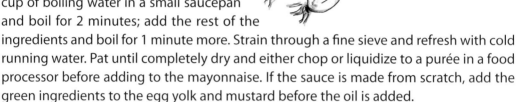

Add spinach and chopped onions to a cup of boiling water in a small saucepan and boil for 2 minutes; add the rest of the ingredients and boil for 1 minute more. Strain through a fine sieve and refresh with cold running water. Pat until completely dry and either chop or liquidize to a purée in a food processor before adding to the mayonnaise. If the sauce is made from scratch, add the green ingredients to the egg yolk and mustard before the oil is added.

MAYONNAISE MOUSSELINE

Add one beaten egg white or a few spoonfuls of whipped cream to 1 cup of mayonnaise.

SAUCE REMOULADE

To 1 cup of mayonnaise add 1 tsp Dijon mustard,1 tsp each of chopped capers and gherkins, 2 tsp chopped fresh herbs, and a few drops of anchovy essence.

MAYONNAISE SUEDOISE

This sauce is perfect with smoked fish.

To 1 cup of mayonnaise add 1 grated apple, 2 tsp of cider vinegar, 2 tsp of grated horseradish and a little salt.

An alternative is to simmer a chopped cooking apple in a little white wine with a sprig of mint, sieve and add to the mayonnaise.

AIOLI

Crush 4 cloves of garlic, having removed the central sprout, into 1egg yolk and, as for mayonnaise, add 1 cup of oil slowly, whisking, to make a thick bowl of sauce. Season with a pinch of salt and serve with boiled fish or cold meats.

A GOOD BASIC SALAD DRESSING

I always have a jar of this made up in the kitchen, to drizzle on sandwiches, into savoury tartlets and, of course, to use on salads.

1tsp of French mustard
100cl white wine vinegar
400cl olive oil
salt and pepper
a clove of garlic, peeled and left whole
a branch of thyme

Mix together until smooth. I make it in a jar and shake it vigorously.

ROUILLE

There are a few versions of this sauce to be served with fish soups, stews and bouillabaisse. This first one is probably the most traditional.

Crush 2 cloves of garlic with 2 small red chilli peppers. Dip a thick slice of crustless white bread into the soup or fish stock and squeeze out the excess. Add to the garlic and pepper. Stir in as if for mayonnaise, whisking well 3 tbsp of olive oil and a little of the fish stock.

For a richer sauce, use 3 cloves garlic with the peppers and add 2 egg yolks. Add a cup of olive oil slowly as if for mayonnaise, and season with Dijon mustard, salt and black pepper.

SAUCE AU BEURRE D'ANCHOIS

I love to serve this sauce as a first course with a variety of crisp fresh vegetables to dip, radishes, celery, cucumber, peppers, fennel and hard boiled egg quarters too.

For the anchovy butter:

6 anchovies

125g butter

For the sauce:

25g butter

a pinch of flour

Dry the anchovies and mash them with the butter. In a small saucepan, melt the 25g of butter, sprinkled with the flour, stir and let this take colour, and then gently incorporate the anchovy butter, stirring over a gentle heat.

BAGNA CAUDA

Another similar sauce to be used the same way. I used to have a special clay dish for this that had a ledge under the bowl for a night light candle to keep the sauce warm in the middle of the table. I am sure I bought it in Italy, but have sadly mislaid it in my travels, although I am sure I could easily replace it now with the power of internet shopping It certainly was a joy on many occasions surrounded by colourful crudités.

200g butter

100g olive oil

1 cup tomato coulis

6 anchovies

4 cloves of garlic

salt and pepper

Place the oil and butter in a small saucepan. Add the anchovies and cook for 10 minutes. Add the tomato coulis and garlic and season. Whisk the sauce, and the oil will incorporate with the tomato to make a smooth sauce. Serve hot.

DEVIL SAUCE
for grilled meats, leftovers or chicken

One of the hardest things at sea was being able to be inspirational with leftovers, to represent food in an unrecognizable guise from a previous meal to please a hungry and often very fussy mix of crew members. This devil sauce was a good tasty solution with leftover roast meat, but also good with grilled chicken or chops.

4 heaped tbsp soft butter

1 heaped tbsp flour

½ cube chicken bouillon

1 tsp dry mustard

a dash of Tabasco

½ tsp ground coriander

1 tsp French mustard

2 tbsp soft mango chutney

1 tbsp Worcester sauce

Butter an oven-to-table dish well

Mash the flour and butter together and mix in the rest of the ingredients until the sauce is spreadable, adding a little more flour if it is too thin. Season and spread on the meat in layers.

If using as a pouring sauce for grilled meats, add some of the sauce to a cup of stock and stir over a moderate heat to make sure the flour is well cooked.

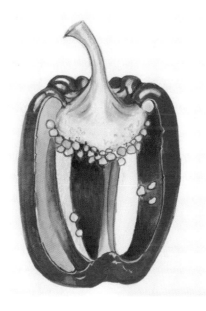

CARIBBEAN SAUCE

Whilst cooking in the islands I mixed up my own sort of local sauce for barbecued meats. Getting all the equipment ashore and organized for a barbeque was always a bit of a nightmare that I came to dread. A meal on board seemed to be the easier option in most cases.

One occasion in particular springs to mind when anchored off a beach in the Bahamas. We loaded the Boston whalers (flat bottomed launches used to ferry to shore) with all the food and grills and set out, dressed in our crisp uniforms, for the beach. On arrival there was a huge swell turning to large breakers as the sea hit the beach so we were already doomed. Leaping out into shoulder deep water in order to avoid the surf further in, we painstakingly unloaded the boats, and managed to take every thing ashore to set up. By now we were a bedraggled team, still faced with the task of fetching the guests.

We began to cook and prepare, setting up trestles for tables, and glasses for wine, when someone noticed we were being observed. Peeping out from the dunes were five huge iguanas. For a moment we considered continuing, but the steady approach of the leader was enough and we frantically began to pack everything away as fast as we possibly could, and to throw it all back in the boats. If nothing else we provided huge entertainment for our guests that day.

1 bunch spring onions
1 red bell pepper
1 green bell pepper
4 large ripe tomatoes
a pinch of pimento
1 large ripe mango
2 cloves of crushed garlic
1 tbsp Worcester sauce
a dash of Tabasco
¼ of fresh pineapple
2 tbsp olive oil
juice of 1 lime
1 tbsp dark brown sugar
1 tbsp Mount Gay rum
grated fresh ginger root

home safe on a blowy day

Finely chop the spring onions and peppers and cook them in the olive oil until softened but not brown. Peel and chop the tomatoes and add to the pepper and onion mix with the crushed garlic, and cook until the tomatoes are a purée. Add the finely-chopped pineapple and mango with all the juice and all the rest of the ingredients, stirring well. Taste and season. Serve with chicken, pork or fish from the barbeque.

BASIC PASTRY, BATTERS, CUSTARDS & CURDS

Before embarking on the sweet section, some basic recipes are needed, to be used time and time again, sometimes adapted a little to suit a particular presentation. What can go wrong if the basic methods are adhered to? The perfect pastry, filled with the perfect crème pâtissière, it would be hard for the strawberries to spoil the result.

In all of my pastries and cakes alike I use unsalted butter, although a good quality soft baking margarine produces good results. If salt is needed I add it separately. I notice in an old French traiteur text book that I acquired from a college in France that their recipes for pastry state 'matière grasse' meaning simply fatty matter, but not actually stating whether it is in fact butter or other. So I will leave this up to the chef, but unsalted butter is my first choice in most recipes unless I state otherwise.

PATE BRISEE

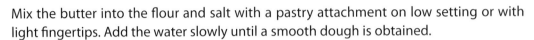

This is the recipe I use for all my savoury tarts and quiches, always pricking and baking it blind until it takes a little colour before filling.

500g flour
200g unsalted butter
1 level tsp salt
enough cold water to mix to a dough which should not be sticky or dry (about 5 tbsp)

Mix the butter into the flour and salt with a pastry attachment on low setting or with light fingertips. Add the water slowly until a smooth dough is obtained.

For a richer dough for meat en croute and meat pies, I substitute 80g of the butter for lard and add 1 beaten egg.

Chill the pastry before rolling.

PATE SABLEE

This is the sweet pastry that I use for all my tart bases and fruit pies. Very short and hard to handle and always better when chilled, this pastry does not take kindly to being rolled more than once, so try to only roll out the required amount to fit the tin.

500g flour
300g unsalted butter
1 egg yolk
100g caster sugar

Mix the butter into the flour and sugar with light fingers or mixer on slow setting until it resembles breadcrumbs. Add the egg yolk and a few drops of lemon juice and mix into a dough. Chill well.

In France I have seen them many times incorporating all the ingredients on a marble slab to help keep it cold, but for my part, I find it easier in a bowl.

PUFF PASTRY

The frozen sort is excellent now but nothing beats home-made when used for mille feuille, palmiers or other lovely sweet treats.

My advice would be make a fairly large quantity and freeze it yourself so you always have some to hand.

500g flour
pinch of salt
500g unsalted butter
240ml cold water
2 tsp lemon juice

Sift the flour and salt. Squeeze the butter to soften and rub 100g into the flour. Make a well in the centre and add the water, mixing well to form a fairly stiff dough.

As soon as the mixture has lost some of its elasticity, roll out into a rectangular shape and place the rest of the butter in the centre. The butter should not be too hard, but should be nearly the same consistency as the dough. Roll out the dough around the butter so it becomes a little thinner, and fold the edges inwards over the butter to make a sealed parcel. Rest for 15 minutes.

Roll out into an oblong 6" x 12" and fold in three. Turn the paste one half move to the right, roll out again into the same oblong shape and fold again. The pastry has now had 2 single turns. Allow to rest in the fridge for 20 minutes and repeat, making 4 more turns. Rest again and turn twice more.

Wrap in cling wrap and refrigerate or freeze until ready to use.

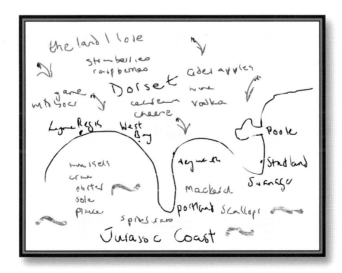

CHOUX PASTRY

So easy to perfect as long as the method is followed carefully.

1 litre water
500g flour
150g unsalted butter
5 eggs

Heat the water in a heavy saucepan and add the butter. When the butter has completely melted and with the mixture just simmering, take off the heat and tip in the sieved flour all at once. Stir thoroughly, making sure no lumps of flour are seen, and then place back on the heat and stir for 5 or 6 minutes to drive off excess moisture from the dough, which should come away cleanly from the sides of the pan.

Allow to cool.

Add the beaten eggs little by little, preferably in the bowl of a food mixer on a slow speed. The mixture will become shiny after a time and when enough egg has been added should form soft peaks that fall over slowly when raised with a wooden spoon. Any remaining beaten egg can be used to glaze your choux buns, profiteroles or éclairs.

The oven temperature is critical, needing to be hot to raise the pastry near 180–200° for the first 20 minutes, but should then be reduced to 150° to harden the pastries for a further 20 minutes. Pierce after coking to release steam and prevent your buns from having a soggy interior.

Choux pastry freezes very well so I bake plenty and freeze my chosen shapes in a plastic box.

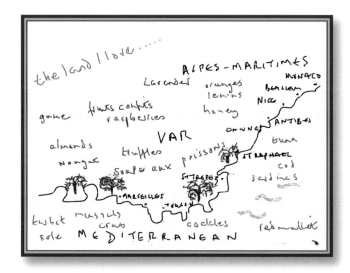

SWEET ALMOND PASTRY

This pastry is very sticky and difficult to roll, being of cake-like consistency, and so needs to be very well chilled.

500g flour
200g caster sugar
500g unsalted butter
1 egg
1 tsp of the finest almond essence

Mix all of the ingredients together thoroughly in the bowl of a food mixer and chill well. Roll out on a cool surface.

BRIOCHES

Croissants are very complicated and not for the inexperienced or faint-hearted cook but brioches, however, are achievable and they make very tasty little breakfast treats, especially with the addition of raisins or chocolate chips Alternatively, they can be stuffed with savoury mixes or pâté as a first course.

Millie's plea
always baking never enough time
for me

500g flour
a pinch of salt
2 tbsp sugar
3 eggs
200ml milk
100g butter
7g of easy bake dried yeast

Sift the flour with the salt and yeast and mix to a dough with the sugar, beaten eggs, and about three quarters of the milk in case the dough is too wet. Add the soft creamed butter last with the rest of the milk if the dough seems dry. Mix really well together. Allow to rise until double in size – I put mine in the fridge for a slow prove overnight, as the cold dough is much easier to handle. Use and shape as desired.

Little brioche moulds are fairly easily available, but little rolls are pretty too. Prove again after kneading and shaping in a warm place and then bake in a moderately hot oven.

BASIC DOUGH FOR WHITE BREAD

700g strong bread flour
1 tsp salt
1 sachet easy bake dried yeast
20g melted butter or 2 tbsp olive oil
250ml warm water

Make a well in the dry ingredients and add the water and oil or butter. Mix with a dough hook and knead on a floured surface. Prove until doubled in size and shape. Bake in a moderately hot oven, the length of cooking time depending on the use of the dough – for rolls about 30 minutes and for a loaf, 40 minutes.

CREME PATISSIERE

This wonderful, creamy custard, so versatile in its uses, is well worth making for yourself even though it is now available ready-made. Some times it is known as Crème Anglaise – English Cream – and I have never really understood why. Maybe that applies to the more liquid version of custard that we pour over crumbles and pies, rather than the very fluffy, thick cream that is the basis for so many of my deserts and tarts. As long as the method is carefully followed it will never curdle or misbehave.

1 litre milk
8 egg yolks
250g caster sugar
60g flour
1 vanilla pod

Mix the egg yolks and sugar together in a large bowl using a hand whisk, until white and creamy. Whisk in the flour, but do not overwork the mixture at this stage.

Bring the milk to the boil with the vanilla pod. When it's really boiling and starting to rise up the pan, pour a little of the hot milk onto the egg mixture, whisking well to amalgamate smoothly before adding the rest of the milk.

Remove the vanilla pod and return the custard to the saucepan. Bring to the boil over a gentle heat, stirring carefully all the time, and cook for 2 minutes until the mixture is thick. Cool and chill.

LEMON CURD

Le Vieux Four recipe for very lemony curd that I use to fill the tarts, lemon meringues, and sponge cakes. It is a good idea to make this quantity, as the curd keeps very well in the fridge or freezer, but of course the quantity is easily halved.

300ml freshly-squeezed lemon juice
225g unsalted butter
200g caster sugar
6 whole eggs plus 2 extra yolks

Put the lemon juice and sugar into the top of a double boiler or into a large bowl over simmering water, and stir until the sugar is dissolved. Add the butter cut into pieces and stir until completely melted. While the butter is melting, whisk the eggs in a bowl until they are completely broken down with little sign of stringy white pieces. Tip the eggs all at once through a fine sieve into the lemon butter mixture, over the hot water, ceaselessly stirring. The mixture will thicken quite quickly and when drops from a wooden spoon remain on top of the curd, it is cooked and should be removed from the heat, cooled and chilled.

TWENTY-TWO YEARS OF BAKING AT
Le Vieux Four

Now I come at last to the sweet section.

When I first opened here in 1991, everyone struggled with my idea; firstly, with the name of the shop itself, which I borrowed from some friends in Antibes with a restaurant of the same name, and secondly with the style and names of the cakes I was baking, for example brioche and clafouti. These items and others are much more familiar now, thanks to television cookery programmes and the growth of super-market wisdom. So little by little I had to woo people into buying my home-made offerings in the French style, and slowly I added more traditional British fine recipes to complete my spread. So the shop grew, as did its popularity, whilst I tried to add a different recipe to the menu every few days, which I still try to achieve now, 22 years later.

Whilst walking around Beaminster church one day with one of the wardens, I noticed a plaque dedicated to 'Henri Le Vieux' of North Street, a serge maker by trade. What bizarre coincidence brought me here, some 200 years later, to reinstate his name above my door, in the very same street? The fireplace that I have recently renovated in the shop may well be the same one that he warmed himself by all those years ago, and this often gives me food for thought.

The Pâtisserie has grown a little since the early days and now fills the whole floor area that the butcher's shop once occupied. With the fireplace exposed in all its glory, I now light the wood burner there in winter and so this delightful space has become our dining room for special occasions and Christmas lunch. Local artists adorn the walls with an ever-changing exhibition of art works, and I am told frequently that the atmosphere is lovely. Good feedback is the best result of all, for cakes and shop alike.

In 1996, '97 and '98, I won several 'Taste of the West' Food Awards, the most prestigious being the Gold Award for my Tartelette au Citron, and I have never been prouder than on seeing the headline which read 'Local Baker Strikes Gold'!

TARTE NORMANDE

A best seller over the years, made with Bramley apples from the tree in the garden at North Street that is at least 50 years old. Normandy, from whence the recipe originated, has the best and thickest double cream I have ever known and, of course, the tastiest butter and richest cheese.

400g of pâte brisée

Line a 10" deep tart tin with a removable base with the pastry, pressing it in with your thumbs to line the flutes on the pan. Roll off the top neatly, prick and bake blind until the pastry is firm to the touch but not brown.

For the filling:

3 or 4 Bramleys

**a few raspberries, blueberries or blackcurrants
to add flavour and colour**

For the batter:

4 heaped tbsp icing sugar

1 heaped tbsp flour

1 egg yolk

500ml double cream

Peel, core and chop the apples into smallish chunks and fill the pastry case with the fruit.

Add the cream and egg yolk to the dry ingredients and whisk well. A little Calvados or brandy goes well in this batter.

Pour over the fruit and bake in a moderate oven for about 30–40 minutes until the batter is firm to the touch, but bake on a fairly low shelf to ensure the pastry does not become over-cooked around the exposed edges. Serve warm.

CLAFOUTI

I think it was Mrs Beeton who wrote that 'a cook should have an air of routine and good discipline about her'. At sea, I always rose at 5am and baked the cake for afternoon tea and prepared the dessert for dinner. Beginning at the end of my menu, so to speak, always seemed to make the day go well for me. In 40 years there is little change to my life then, I still rise at 5am and bake cakes, but thankfully my kitchen is stable and predictable.

300g puff pastry

Roll out the pastry fairly thinly to line a 10" shallow tart tin with a removable base. Prick the base of the tart and fill with stoned black cherries.

For the batter:
2 heaped tbsp of icing sugar
1 level tbsp flour
1 egg yolk
300ml double cream

Whisk the cream and egg yolk into the dry ingredients with the addition of a dash of kirsch if liked.

Bake in a moderately hot oven for 30–35 minutes until the batter is golden brown, making sure the pastry base is cooked sufficiently. Ovens vary, and I find that this pie bakes best in my fan-assisted electric oven on a central shelf.

Serve warm.

LEMON, CHOCOLATE & FRUIT TARTELETTES

Roll out just enough pâte brisée to fill the tins of your choice, a large one for several people for a dinner party perhaps, individual ones for tea, or tiny ones to be part of a selection of petit fours.

Bake blind in a moderate oven until the cases are softly brown and cool on a rack. The pastry should be like shortbread with a crisp bite.

Do not fill until a few hours before they are needed; the cases store very well for a couple of days in a tin. Once they are filled they must be refrigerated to keep the base crisp.

Fruit and crème pâtissière

Make a glaze with sieved apricot jam mixed with a little water and brought to the boil to melt. Brush the inside of the tart shell with this before filling with an even layer of crème. Arrange your fruits of choice carefully and brush with the heated glaze.

tarte aux abricots et myrtilles

Lemon

Pipe homemade lemon curd into the tart shell using a wide star nozzle. Decorate with a glazed lemon slice.

Chocolate

For the filling for six 4" tartlets or one 10" tart:

Melt 400g of best Belgian cooking chocolate over hot water. Add 280ml of double cream and stir until smoothly amalgamated with the chocolate. Allow to cool until the mixture starts to thicken but is still soft enough to pipe into the shells. Fill the tarts neatly and chill; dust with cocoa powder if liked, or chocolate shavings.

COEURS D'AMANDE

I have been making these little cakes every day since I opened, and I have to say they are probably the most consistently popular pastry I have ever made.

If you cannot find 6 little heart-shaped tins like mine, 6 ordinary 4" tartlet tins will do.

Take 300g of sweet almond pastry (see page 81) and line the tins, carefully. Put a good dollop of strawberry jam in each, and roll out a lid, placing the pastry completely over the tin and then roll over it with the rolling pin to both cut off the excess and seal in the jam. Brush with beaten egg to glaze and bake in a moderate oven for 20–25 minutes until golden brown. Cool a little, remove from the tins and serve warm.

GATEAU BASQUE

I found these in practically every artisan bakery that I visited in the Basque region and, alongside the almond hearts, have also become a best-seller.

I make them in 5" tins but the choice is yours, although the bigger the tin the harder it is to ensure that the base is cooked right through.

Proceed exactly the same as for the hearts, but this time fill the tartlets with crème pâtissière. Roll and seal the pastry carefully to keep the crème inside. Bake until golden and serve warm.

BELGIAN CHOCOLATE BROWNIES

The original recipe for these, I have to admit, came from a rather scruffy little cookbook that I picked up in St Lucia, aptly titled Cookbook St Lucie. It appears that quite a few of the ladies on the island contributed to this little manual, as each recipe bears their name – Nancy's saucy pork chops, Betty Ann's pork pie and Cathie's coconut jelly, to name just a few. The brownies, however are just called Mother's brownies and from these mine were born.

I met an old man who used to sell us vegetables in Fort Lauderdale and he grew the biggest avocados I have ever seen, and with his addiction to my brownies, we were able to barter for many months.

200g butter
200g dark Belgian chocolate
250g caster sugar
3 large eggs
100g self raising flour

Melt the butter and chocolate together in a saucepan until smooth. Do not allow to boil. Whisk the eggs and sugar together and stir into the chocolate mixture, stirring well. Lastly, stir in the sifted flour carefully, ensuring that there are no pockets or lumps of flour.

Line a baking tin 8" x 6" and pour in the mixture. The brownies should be about an inch thick. Bake for 20–25 minutes in a moderate oven until set, but do not overcook or the brownies will be dry.

For the icing:
150g dark chocolate
125ml double cream

Melt the chocolate in a double boiler and add the cream, stirring well. Allow to cool and thicken a little, and then spread over the cooled tray of brownies. Sprinkle with cocoa powder.

GATEAU AUX POMMES ET AUX AMANDES

I suppose this is my own version of Dorset apple cake with a French twist, although I do make a more traditional version as well. This one, which I usually bake in a round sponge cake tin, is wonderful with a big dollop of crème frâiche or thick yogurt, served up while still warm from the oven. The grated apple keeps this cake deliciously moist.

125g butter
125g caster sugar
3 eggs
125g ground almonds
1 heaped tbsp self raising flour
1 peeled and grated Bramley apple
1 tbsp flaked almonds

Cream the butter and sugar until white and fluffy. Add the beaten eggs alternately with the flour and almonds, followed by the grated apple.

Butter and line an 8" sandwich tin and fill evenly with the mixture. Scatter the flaked almonds on the top and bake for 20–25 minutes until brown, risen and set. Cool and sprinkle with icing sugar.

LEMON DIPPED GINGER CAKE

If the truth were known, I was never very good at ginger cake until quite recently, when at last I seem to have got to grips with perfecting a moist, gingery texture. I also found a new tin, which renewed my enthusiasm, and little lemon dipped ginger cakes were accomplished and admired.

The tin is a heavy non-stick tray with loose bottomed indentations for 12 miniature sponge cakes or similar, very useful, but fiddly, for cheesecakes too. I line the tin with a band of baking parchment so that the cakes can rise up above the edge of the tin without losing their shape. This recipe makes either 7 little cakes and one loaf cake 8" x 5", or 2 of the latter.

125g butter
125g dark brown sugar
125g black treacle
125g golden syrup
a piece fresh ginger
2 eggs
225ml milk
300g self raising flour

Melt the butter, sugar and treacles ingredients together in a heavy bottomed pan on a low heat, and stir until smooth. Grate in about a tablespoon of peeled fresh ginger. Whisk the eggs in the milk and add to the mixture, and lastly beat in the sifted flour, mixing well.

Pour into the selected tins, using parchment liners for the loaf tins. Bake in the centre of a moderate oven for 30–40 minutes until risen and firm to the touch. Obviously, if you have used individual tins they bake in half the time.

Make a glacé icing with icing sugar and lemon juice and dip the small, cooled cakes to give them a lemon lid. Spread remaining icing on the loaf cake.

FLORENTINES

I began to make Florentines for the shop in response to a request for a gluten-free coffee-time treat. If you add a little flour they hold together more satisfactorily, but without they still are perfectly successful.

My Florentines are always a bit more on the generous side compared to those you might find in a packet.

For 12:
225g flaked almonds
125g chopped peel
125g glacé cherries
30g butter
2 tbsp caster sugar
140ml double cream
½ tbsp flour (optional)
200g dark chocolate

In a saucepan, melt the butter with the sugar to a smooth paste, adding the flour at this point, if used, to make a roux. Add the cream gradually, and mix well. Lastly, add all the fruit and nuts.

Place tablespoonfuls of the mixture onto a lined baking tray, spreading into flat, roundish shapes. Bake in a fairly hot oven until golden brown. Mine take about 15 minutes. Allow to cool on the tray and when they have hardened, flip them over with a palette knife and spread melted chocolate on the flat underside. Chill until the chocolate is hard.

LEMON DRIZZLE CAKE WITH THYME & LEMON BALM

The perfect summer cake.

200g butter
200g sugar
100g ground almonds
100g self raising flour
4 eggs
zest of 1 lemon
2 tsp fresh thyme leaves
1 tsp chopped fresh lemon balm

thyme

Grease and line a 9" loose-bottomed tin. Cream together the butter and sugar until fluffy. Add the beaten egg, almonds and flour alternately and finally add the lemon zest and herbs. Spoon into the tin and bake in moderate oven until risen and golden brown.

For the drizzle:
3 tbsp icing sugar
juice of 2 lemons
2 tbsp water
1 tsp thyme leaves
1 tsp lemon balm chopped

Reduce the drizzle until syrupy. Prick the cake with a fork while still warm and pour over the syrup. Decorate with flowers from the herbs.

FAR BRETON AUX PRUNEAUX
(with Black Cow vodka)

In West Dorset we are proud to have an extremely innovative farmer, who, with a little help from his friends, has managed to turn milk products into vodka. I have used this smooth delight here and there in my recipes with very palatable results.

300g pâte brisée
¾ litre milk
1 vanilla pod
2 eggs
100g sugar
75g flour
2 tbsp Black Cow Vodka
10g butter
150g prunes, destoned
a few raspberries

Butter a 10" quiche tin and line with pâte brisée. Bake blind until firm but not brown. Bring the milk to the boil in a saucepan with the vanilla pod. Whisk the eggs with the sugar until foamy, and add the flour, mixing well. Strain the milk into the custard and add the vodka.

Stir over a low heat until the mixture becomes thick and pour into the pastry base. Drop the prunes into the custard and scatter in the few raspberries. Bake in a moderate oven for 30–35 minutes until the custard is set. Serve warm or chilled.

Far Breton

BLOOD ORANGE CHEESECAKE

I adore cheesecake, one of my big weaknesses. People always say, 'how can you not eat all that you bake?' The answer is I do eat it all, but I do have my favourites. I like cheesecake of the chilled variety as opposed to the baked variety, to be quite tart in flavour and the juice of blood oranges give just that, in the right degree with the addition of a little lemon juice to make it really zingy.

In a 9" loose-bottomed tin, make a base with digestives crushed in the food processor with melted butter. I use about 10 biscuits with 60g melted butter. Pack this down hard with the back of a wooden spoon, and chill.

For the filling:
200g soft cream cheese
200g crème pâtissière
100ml softly whipped double cream
juice and zest of 2 blood oranges
juice of 1 lemon
3 leaves gelatine

Dissolve the gelatine in the fruit juices, either in the microwave or in a bowl over hot water. Stir and make sure it has completely dissolved. Beat together the cream cheese and custard until there are no lumps of cheese visible. Stir in the gelatine mixture and the zest. Chill until beginning to set and finally fold in the cream. Pour onto the biscuit base and chill until set.

Decorate with slices of blood orange and fresh lemon balm.

ROULADE AU CHOCOLAT

In quite a few of my desert cake recipes, I use a Genoise sponge which is made with very little butter or sometimes none at all, making the texture very light. A customer once observed to me that the best thing about my roulade was the ratio of sponge to cream, and I think he meant that the sponge was thin and light compared to the ample amount of fresh chocolate cream it was encasing. Roulades are always tricky to roll – baking parchment helps – but anyway, if it looks a bit homemade then the outer layer of cream conceals all.

Line a 9" x 12" baking tray with baking parchment

2 eggs
80g sugar
50g self raising flour
30g cocoa powder

Whisk the eggs with the sugar in the bowl of an electric mixer until a thick, white, mousse like consistency is achieved.

Carefully fold in the sifted flour and cocoa with a spatula, trying to keep the mixture light and airy. Spread into the tray and bake in a moderate oven for 15–20 minutes until firm to the touch.

Turn the sponge out onto a piece of parchment and peel off the paper. Brush the sponge with a brandy syrup made by reducing 2 tablespoons of brandy with 4 tablespoons of water and 2 tablespoons of caster sugar.

Softly whip 100ml of double cream with a scant tablespoon of icing sugar and 3 teaspoons of cocoa. Spread the cream over the Genoise and carefully roll, using the paper beneath to help.

Cover the outside of your roulade with whipped cream with a little icing sugar added, and decorate with chocolate curls, grated chocolate or crushed meringue sprinkled with cocoa.

This recipe can be varied by adding coffee essence to the sponge instead of cocoa, bringing the flour up to 80g to maintain the same consistency, thus making a mocha roulade.

Sometimes I add finely chopped hazelnuts to the cream in the centre and decorate the outside with them, creating a hazelnut roulade.

GATEAU AU CHOCOLAT TRUFFE

This cake makes a wonderful birthday cake for chocoholics, when more of a desert is needed rather than a simple teatime sponge.

A few years ago I did make three of varying sizes for a wedding and decorated with chocolate leaves and white fresh flowers. They looked superb, and although I was a little worried about the warmth of the day, apparently they held up until serving.

Grease and line a 10" loose-bottomed cake tin

3 eggs
120g sugar
75g self raising flour
50g cocoa powder

Use the same method as in the preceding recipe to make the Genoise and bake for 30–40 minutes until risen and firm to the touch. Turn onto a rack to cool. When the cake is cold, cut carefully into 3 layers with a serrated knife. Brush each layer with brandy syrup and reassemble the cake, sandwiched with chocolate cream.

For the ganache or truffle icing:
Melt 300g of dark fine chocolate in a double boiler until smooth. Add 200ml of double cream and stir until completely smoothly mixed with the chocolate. Leave the ganache to cool but not harden, so that it can be easily spread on the top and sides of the cake. Any remaining can be piped with a star nozzle around the edge.

Decorate with chocolate shavings, or home made chocolate leaves. I find that strawberry plant leaves work well; simply paint them with melted chocolate, chill and when the chocolate is hard it is easy to peel off the leaf, but it must be quickly done with a cool hand. Dust with cocoa powder.

Chill the finished cake, but take out of the fridge 1 hour before serving to prevent the ganache from cracking when it is cut.

GATEAU MANQUE A L'ORANGE ET AU COINTREAU, GARNITURE AU CHOCOLAT

This is a delicious orange-flavoured Genoise cake with Cointreau and a chocolate icing that I saw in a French magazine and modified a little, and it turned out to be a very grand cake for maybe a special birthday tea.

Butter and line a 10" loose-bottomed cake tin

For the Genoise:

3 oranges

70g butter

3 eggs

150g sugar

150g self raising flour

2 tbsp Cointreau

Squeeze 1 orange and grate the zest. Melt 50g of the butter and cool.

Separate the eggs, and whisk the yolks with the sugar. Add the juice and zest of the orange, the melted butter and the flour. Mix until a smooth batter and fold in the stiffly-beaten egg whites. Pour into the tin and bake for 35–40 minutes. Take out of the tin and cool on a rack.

For the icing and filling:

2 eggs

200g dark chocolate

100g butter

6 tbsp sugar

grated zest of half an orange

Separate the eggs. Melt the chocolate and butter in a double boiler. Off the heat, add the sugar, orange zest and egg yolks, and mix well. Whip the egg whites and fold them in carefully. Leave to harden in the refrigerator.

Cut the cake in two, then brush the 2 halves with Cointreau. Fill the cake and reassemble and ice the top, finally decorating with thin slices of orange.

BAVAROIS AU CASSIS

In the summer when there are wonderful soft fruits about, even in my garden if the birds do not get there first, fresh fruit bavarois are quite easy to make and look very accomplished when decorated with fresh berries and herbs.

Butter and line a 9" loose-bottomed tin

For the Genoise base:

1 egg

40g sugar

40g self raising flour

½ tsp vanilla essence

Whisk the egg with the sugar until white and frothy, add the essence and carefully fold in the flour. Spread the mixture in the tin and bake in a moderately hot oven until firm and brown. Cool on a rack and reline the tin, placing the now cooled cake back in to form the base.

225g fresh blackcurrants

90g sugar

150ml water

3 leaves gelatine

300ml double cream

3 egg whites

Top and tail the blackcurrants and cook them in a little of the water with a tablespoon of sugar until soft. Pass them through a nylon sieve. Make syrup with the rest of the water and sugar, allow to cool until warm and dissolve the gelatine in this liquid. Add the fruit pulp and the softly-whipped cream and place in the fridge until half set. Fold in the stiffly-beaten egg whites and spread the mousse evenly over the sponge base. Chill until set and decorate with a sprig of fresh blackcurrants and edible leaves such as lemon balm.

PETIT FOURS

Petit Fours, just literally 'small things from the oven', are without a doubt fiddly to produce, but like good canapé they really demonstrate the attention to detail and innovativeness of a first-class cook, so even a small selection is really worth the effort.

Madeleines

Butter a non-stick Madeleine tray (makes about 12)

75g butter
100g sugar
3 eggs
100g self raising flour
some drops of orange flower water
icing sugar

Cream the butter and sugar and add the beaten eggs, followed by the sifted flour and orange water. Bake in a hot oven until golden brown.

Cool on a rack and sprinkle with icing sugar.

Mrs Robinson's Almond and Honey Madeleines

Reminiscent, fleetingly, of my old St Lucien cook book where every recipe has a name at the top, these are my dear friend Sue Robinson's.

4 egg whites
75g self raising flour
250g icing sugar
125g ground almonds
2 tbsp honey
½ tsp almond essence
grated zest of 1 lemon
175g butter

Melt the butter in a saucepan with the sugar, honey, zest and essence. Add the flour and ground almonds, mixing well and lastly fold in the stiffly-beaten egg whites. Bake in a hot oven until golden brown and transfer to a cooling rack.

Macarons de Nancy

250g icing sugar
125g ground almonds
3 egg whites

Mix the sugar and the almonds and fold in the stiffly-beaten whites.

Place the mixture in little piles with a teaspoon on a lined baking tray. Flatten with the back of a teaspoon dipped in cold water. Bake in a moderately hot oven for 15 minutes and transfer to a rack to cool.

Chaussons mignons

Chaussons translate as slippers, and these are cute ones as the name suggests!

400g puff pastry
jam or almond cream
1 egg
flaked almonds
sugar

Roll out the pastry to about ½ cm thickness and cut little squares of 8cm. Place a teaspoon of jam or almond cream in the centre and fold the four corners towards the centre. Seal firmly and brush with egg. Sprinkle with sugar and flaked almonds. Bake in a moderately hot oven for 10–15 minutes.

For the almond cream, mix together 40g ground almonds, 5cl crème frâiche, 30g sugar and 1 egg.

Torsades

I love to spend the day making all these little delicacies and when I finish this book I think petit four afternoons at *Le Vieux Four* could be fun.

300g puff pastry
1 egg yolk to glaze
sugar
flaked almonds

Roll the pastry to ½ cm. Brush with beaten egg and cut into bands 2cm x 8cm. Sprinkle with sugar and flaked almonds.

Twist the bands like a corkscrew, place on a damp baking sheet and cook in a moderately hot oven for 10 minutes.

Coquins

These biscuits are called coquins, which translated means mischievous, and like miniature jammy dodgers, they certainly add interest to any platter of petit fours.

120g sugar
a pinch of salt
1 egg
220g flour
25g ground almonds
125g butter
1 tsp cinnamon
125g raspberry or strawberry jam
50g icing sugar

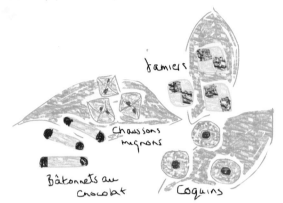

Mix together the egg, sugar, salt, flour, cinnamon and ground almonds. Add the butter, cut in small pieces, and mix in with your finger tips, gradually forming a dough. Chill for one hour.

Roll out to a thickness of 2 or 3mm and cut 4cm circles with a pastry cutter. Cut a round hole in the centre of half of the discs about 1cm diameter.

Cook the biscuits for about 6–7 minutes in a moderately hot oven and cool. Attach the tops to the bottoms with jam and sprinkle with icing sugar.

Damiers

These little biscuits named Damiers, the French word for draughts, look tricky but actually they are fairly simple. On long Atlantic crossings when the weather allowed the galley to be fairly stable, I would amuse myself with recipes such as these, which were always greatly appreciated from a tin on the bridge for the long night watches. On one such voyage on a wooden ketch, we had a problem with a leaky deck right above the galley, but I managed to wedge an umbrella to protect my endangered biscuits as they cooled, which caused much merriment and raised the spirits of the whole crew.

250g self raising flour
150g butter
100g sugar
a few drops of vanilla essence
a pinch of salt
1 tbsp water
30g of cocoa powder

Sieve the flour, make a well in the centre and add the sugar, salt, vanilla and water. Mix into half the surrounding flour, then add the butter in small pieces, kneading all together quickly. Split the dough into 2 parts and add the chocolate powder to one half. Chill the two mixes, wrapped separately. ×2
So you have 2× choc, 2× plain
Roll each part into the shape of a sausage and push firmly together either pressing into a round shape or square. Chill for one hour, roll the dough carefully in sugar and cut into slices of 8–10mm. Bake in a moderately hot oven until they begin to brown, 12–15 minutes, and transfer to a cooling tray.

4 g aola I

Most of these petit fours are the perfect accompaniment to ice cream, but the next two biscuits are particularly mouth-watering.

Spritz au chocolat

200g butter
120g sugar
1 egg white
250g flour
2 level tsp baking powder
50g cocoa powder
50g ground almonds

sugar

Work the butter until soft and add the flour and lightly-beaten egg white. Mix in the flour, baking powder, chocolate and ground almonds. Place the mixture in a piping bag with a large star nozzle and pipe into small batons or S shapes on parchment paper. Bake in a moderately hot oven for 15 minutes.

Tuiles

250g flaked almonds
250g sugar
4 egg whites
40g flour

In a bowl, mix the almonds, sugar and flour. Moisten with the lightly-beaten egg white to make a thick dough. With the aid of 2 teaspoons, place in little heaps on baking parchment and cook in a moderately hot oven for 8–10 minutes. Move them quickly with a wide palette knife onto a rolling pin or a tube to give them a curled shape as they set.

Batonnets

200g flour
a pinch of salt
2 tsp baking powder
125g of sugar
1 egg
100g butter
a few drops of vanilla essence

To decorate:
75g of flaked almonds
3 tbsp sieved apricot jam
100g chocolate
a nut of butter

Make a well in the mixture of flour and baking powder. Add the sugar, the salt, the egg yolk and half the egg white. Mix in with half of the surrounding flour, then add the butter cut into small pieces and knead into a ball. Leave to rest for an hour.

Roll out to 3mm thickness and cut into batons roughly 2cm x 6cm. Place on a lined baking sheet and brush with the rest of the egg white and sprinkle with flaked almonds.

Bake in a moderately hot oven for 10 minutes and cool.

Melt the chocolate in a double boiler. Brush the batons with the warm apricot jam and dip the ends into the melted chocolate, and place on a tray to set.

SEASONAL RECIPES AND
A FEW *Le Vieux Four* FAVOURITES

There have not been many festive holidays over the last 40 years when I have not been cooking. I can remember swimming ashore on Paradise Island in the West Indies on Christmas Day, and although I had had a hard, long day, I thought I was the luckiest person alive. Serving up a turkey in tropical climes always seems strange, but the carol singers in the boats sailing out to greet us spun a magic that was unforgettable. The guests would laugh at the inevitable splash after dinner when the cook hit the water from the bow.

Easter and Christmas at *Le Vieux Four* are busy times – all those puddings, cakes and hot cross buns – but the feedback over the following weeks makes it all worth while every time. Some of my customers have ordered my Christmas fare for over 20 years now, and thinking about my handiwork on all of their festive tables makes me very proud, grateful and fulfilled.

BEAMINSTER BUNS

The Beaminster Bun evolved from my Hot Cross Buns, which when I first made them were an unexpected success, being slightly heavy and yeasty compared to the supermarket variety. They became so popular that I made them without the crosses at other times of the year, donating a small amount of each sale to our local cancer hospice. I feel they are a winter recipe when we need to put on a few extra pounds to help keep us warm, through the dark, cold, short days, always to be served warm or toasted with lashings of butter.

Makes 24 buns:
1½kg flour
5 eggs
120g butter
550ml milk
2 tbsp mixed spice
100g sultanas
100g currants
60g mixed peel
2 sachets easy bake dried yeast
1tsp salt

Put the flour, salt, yeast and spice into the bowl of your mixer fitted ready with a dough hook. Make a well in the centre and add the milk warmed with the softened butter, and the eggs. Mix well until starting to form a dough and, lastly, add the fruit. Keep mixing all the ingredients until a smooth consistency is reached; it should not be too sticky. Turn out onto a floured surface and continue to knead by hand. Place back in the bowl, cover with cling film and prove until doubled in size. I put mine in the refrigerator overnight for a slow prove, then knock it back and shape into buns, proving again, this time in a warm place until doubled in size again and ready to bake.

For the crosses:

Mix 2 tablespoons of flour with a tablespoon of icing sugar and with enough milk to form a thick paste. Pipe crosses on the buns and bake in a moderately hot oven until risen and brown. Brush with a sieved apricot jam glaze as they come out of the oven to give them a sticky, tasty glow.

LAVENDER SCONES

I have never really been very proud of my attempts at scones until recently when my elderly father developed a continuous need for them, which caused me to make more of an effort, and the addition of various flavours from the garden made a transformation of the ordinary scone into something special.

For about 8–10:

225g self raising flour

1 level tsp baking powder

40g soft butter

30g caster sugar

1 egg

150ml milk

2 tsp dried lavender flowers

Rub the butter into the dry ingredients and stir in the sugar and lavender. Whisk the egg into the milk and add to the dry ingredients mixing to a soft dough. Roll or pat out to a thickness of about three-quarters of an inch and use a fluted cutter to make small scones. Brush with milk and bake in a moderately hot oven for 10–15 minutes until golden brown.

Cool on a wire rack and serve warm.

DUNDEE CAKE

A favourite cake for the store cupboard, never waning in popularity all year round.

For two 8" cakes:

300g sultanas

300g currants

100g glacé cherries

100g mixed peel

grated rind of 1 orange

Leave the fruit to steep overnight in 2 tbsp of whisky

300g butter

300g caster sugar

300g self raising flour

300g flour

6 eggs

2 tsp mixed spice

grated nutmeg

Cherries and or nuts to decorate

Cream the butter and sugar, whisk the eggs and add them alternately with the flour, mixing thoroughly. Add the spice, nutmeg and grated orange zest, followed by all the dried fruit. Share the mixture carefully between 2 lined cake tins and decorate the tops with a few cherries or nuts. The secret to keeping the cake moist is to cook slowly, so mine go in the middle of my big gas oven on the lowest setting, which would be about 100°C. This bakes them perfectly in around 3 hours. Take them out when risen and brown and a cake tester comes out clean, and cool in the tin.

Wrapped well, these cakes will keep for 3 weeks or so in a cool place.

BISHOP'S CAKE

I first learnt to make this cake whilst studying for my diploma in London and then I quite forgot about it for years until the idea of putting chocolate into a fruit cake jumped into my head and I realized I had encountered this before with the Bishop's Cake, a moist fruity chocolatey concoction.

For 2 loaf cakes, using parchment liners:

the weight of 4 eggs in self raising flour, butter and brown sugar
100g chocolate, grated, or cooking chocolate in chips
75g sultanas
50g glacé cherries
30g candied peel
½ tsp each of cinnamon, ginger and nutmeg

Cream the butter and three quarters of the sugar, add the egg yolks and cream again. Beat the egg whites to froth and fold them into the rest of the sugar. Add the whites and the flour alternately to the creamy butter mixture, and then fold in the rest of the ingredients. Bake in a moderately hot oven for about 30–40 minutes. The cakes should be moist in the middle.

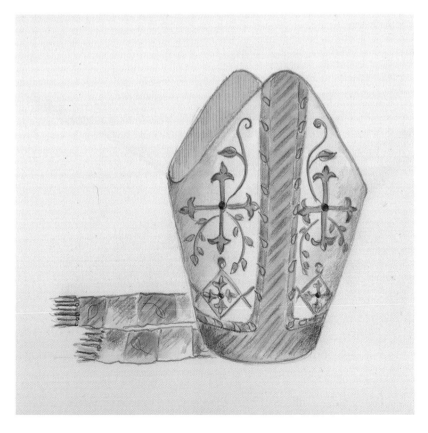

SIMNEL CAKE

Butter and line a 10" deep cake tin

300g currants

300g sultanas

75g peel

75g glacé cherries

Place the dried fruits in a bowl overnight with 2 tbsp of brandy

300g butter

300g soft light brown sugar

1 tbsp golden syrup

5 eggs

½ tbsp mixed spice

500g golden marzipan

350g flour

Cream the butter and sugar, whisk the eggs and add alternately with the flour. Mix in the fruits, spice and syrup, making sure all the ingredients are well blended. Place half the mixture in the prepared tin, and roll out and place a layer of marzipan about 3mm thick. Sandwich this with the rest of the cake mix. Place a round of baking parchment on the cake to keep the top flat.

Bake in a very slow oven at about 100°C until the cake is brown and firm to the touch. A cake tester is not a good tool for this cake as the marzipan in the middle will always be sticky while the cake is hot.

Allow the cake to get completely cold before decorating. Roll out a round of marzipan to fit the top of the cake and make 11 marzipan eggs. Using a cook's blow torch, scorch the marzipan and eggs carefully. Using a little glacé icing, fix the eggs on the top of the marzipan-covered cake. The violets in the garden always time their arrival perfectly and so I crystallize some for the top of the cakes, dipping them in egg white, sprinkling with sugar and placing them to dry on the back of the Aga a few days before I need them.

Le Vieux Four **CHRISTMAS CAKE**

A simple, no-frills cake that has never failed to please The secret of the moist, juiciness of the crumb lies in the long, slow cooking – I cook mine on the lowest shelf of the gas oven with the setting on the warming oven star.

Butter and line a 10" deep cake tin

700g currants
100g peel
225g raisins
225g sultanas
100g glacé cherries
3 tbsp brandy
350g flour
350g dark brown sugar
350g butter
4 eggs
1½ tbsp black treacle
1 tbsp mixed spice
½ tsp grated nutmeg
grated rind of 2 oranges and 1 lemon

Soak the dried fruit overnight in the brandy. Cream the butter and sugar and add the eggs alternately with a little flour to prevent curdling, before adding the rest of the flour. All the fruit, spices, and grated peel should now be added and, lastly, the treacle. Make sure everything is well mixed in before spreading into the prepared tin.

Cover the cake with a circle of Bakewell paper to fit with a snip in the centre to release the steam. Bake at a very low temperature for 4 hours or until a cake tester comes out clean and the cake is firm to the touch.

Cool in the tin.

Le Vieux Four MINCEMEAT

This recipe makes a big batch of mincemeat to last a family over Christmas, and perhaps some to put in jars as a gift. I warm mine through in a warm oven to melt the suet, which coats the apple and stops fermentation during storage. I usually make six or seven batches when the Bramleys are ready on the tree in September, to mature for Christmas, and if there is any left it is stored in the fridge and used the following year, being even better for the keeping. Of course these quantities can be halved.

1.5kg Bramley apples; peeled, cored and chopped into small pieces
700g vegetarian suet
700g sultanas
700g raisins
700g currants
700g peel
1kg dark brown sugar
grated peel of 2 oranges and 2 lemons
12 tsp mixed spice
18 tbsp brandy

Mix all the ingredients together (excluding the brandy) in a large pan that will fit in your oven. I inherited several large preserving pans that are perfect for this purpose.

Place the pan in the oven on its very lowest setting, and stir every now and then to make sure nothing is burning at the bottom. When the suet has melted, take the mincemeat out and stir in the brandy. Keep stirring from time to time as the mincemeat cools to distribute the suet throughout the mixture. Store in the fridge.

Le Vieux Four CHRISTMAS PUDDING

This recipe will make four 500g basins. It is much more practical to make two years worth at once, for the cooking and mixing is a little laborious. I never have Christmas puddings to store as customers buy them in the New Year to keep for the following Christmas, and they always assure me they mature beautifully.

200g vegetarian suet
100g self raising flour
2 tbsp mixed spice
2 tsp grated nutmeg
450g dark brown sugar
225g sultanas
225g raisins
600g currants
50g peel
2 large Bramleys; peeled, cored and chopped
grated peel of 2 oranges and 2 lemons
4 eggs
4 tbsp brandy
600ml Guinness
200g white breadcrumbs

Mix all of the dry ingredients thoroughly, ticking them off as you go along to make sure nothing is forgotten, and lastly add the eggs, Guinness and brandy. Stir, making sure there are no pockets of any single ingredient. Distribute between the basins and put a layer of baking parchment under the lid.

Steam the puddings over boiling water for at least 4 hours until the colour turns almost black. They should only need an hour's steaming to warm through on Christmas Day. Turn out and flame with a little warm brandy.

'The experienced housekeeper knows that early rising is one of the secrets of successful management. There is no work like morning work, particularly household tasks, and those we take up early in the day, when fresh from a night's rest and a good breakfast are "trifles light as air" in comparison with the same dragged or hurried through later when there is not time for their proper performance.'

Mrs Beeton

Bibliography

Caribbean Cookery, Elisabeth Lambert Oritiz; Penguin Books 1973
Complete Cookery Course, Delia Smith; Book Club Associates 1979
Cook Book St Lucie, Betty Anne Cook; Voice Press 1976
Fish Cookery, Jane Grigson; International Wine and Food Publishing 1973
The Food of Greece, Vilma Liccouras Chontilles; Crown 1979
French Provincial Cooking, Elizabeth David; Michael Joseph 1965
Guide Cuisine; Prisma Presse 1990
How to be a Domestic Goddess, Nigella Lawson; Condé Nast Publications 2000
La Cuisine Française, Marie-Claude Bisson; Solar 1982
La Petite Cuisine, Lyn Hall; Cookery School 1976
La Vraie Cuisine de nos Provinces, Paulette Buteux; Nathan 1984
Larousse Gastrominique, Prosper Montagne; Hamlyn 1961
Le Compagnon Traiteur, J Charette; Jerome Vilette 1989
Les Desserts, M. Philippe Conticini ; Solar 2001
Les Petits Fours, Ingershiem; Colmar 1981
Mrs Beeton's Everyday Cookery; Ward, Lock and Co Ltd
New British Classics, Gary Rhodes; The Book People Ltd 2000
Tartes Sucrees et Salees, Alessandra Avallone; Solar 1991

INDEX

Note: recipe titles are not included in the index as they are listed in the Contents pages.